WHAT A HAZARD
A LETTER IS

What a Hazard a Letter is

The Strange Destiny of the Unsent Letter

Caroline Atkins

SAFE HAVEN

For my mother, who would have had so many ideas to contribute

First published 2018 by
Safe Haven Books Ltd
12 Chinnocks Wharf
42 Narrow Street
London E14 8DJ
www.safehavenbooks.co.uk

A catalogue record for this book is available from the British Library.

ISBN 978 0 9932911 7 3

10 9 8 7 6 5 4 3 2 1

2022 2021 2020 2019 2018

Typeset in Filosofia and Mrs Eaves by SX Composing DTP, Rayleigh, Essex
Printed and bound in the UK by Clays Ltd, Elcograf S.p.A.

What a Hazard a Letter is?
When I think of the Hearts it has scuttled and sunk,
I almost fear to lift my Hand
to so much as a Superscription

Emily Dickinson, from a letter to
Thomas Wentworth Higginson, 6 August 1885

Contents

Introduction

It was Janet Malcolm who started this. Towards the end of her wonderful book *The Silent Woman*, about the relationship between Sylvia Plath and Ted Hughes, she talks about writing a letter, to a fellow biographer, that she decided after deliberation not to send, and in an intriguing aside comments that the genre of the unsent letter would make an interesting subject for further study. She doesn't quite say, 'Someone should write a book about it,' but she does point out, 'We have all contributed to it.'

And we have. *I* have. Going back through old diaries, I found several that I never sent, two of them (including one in turquoise ink) dating back nearly 30 years, and all written so neatly that I must have copied them out several times to produce a draft I was happy with, yet still not posted . . . So Janet Malcolm's suggestion got me thinking, and this book is the result.

For Malcolm, letters provide the archaeology of our former feelings, revealing the past with vivid accuracy. Read one sent to you 20 years ago, and it takes you straight back to a specific moment in your life. Read one that you *wrote* 20 years ago, and it's like a shortcut to your former self. It's why letters are so sought after by biographers, and why they can prove such a minefield, exposing minds and motives unfiltered by interpretation. If historical figures could read their own biographies, there would be plenty they wished they hadn't sent, or even written in the first place.

But where Janet Malcolm sees letters as unlocking the past, the poet Emily Dickinson frets about their potential to wreak havoc in the future. For her they are live ammunition, each one capable of lobbing a grenade into our lives by delivering – or discovering – momentous news. 'What a Hazard a Letter is?' she wrote to a friend in August 1885: eager, yet at the same time fearful, for news of a mutual acquaintance who was dangerously ill. 'When I think of the Hearts it has scuttled and sunk, I almost fear to lift my Hand to so much as a Superscription.' In the words of another of her poems, 'We must be careful what we say. No bird resumes its egg.' Once we've read a letter, we can't 'unread' it, so each one we send becomes another hostage to fortune.

And between the wariness of revealing too much and the fear of provoking trouble to come, we can lose the confidence to send what we've written.

Of course, our correspondence these days is so disposable that, of the dozens of texts and emails we compose every day, we regularly leave a good number unsent just because events move so fast (although, paradoxically, it's also far too easy to press the 'Send' button and fire off a message accidentally, and we've even invented a specific term – trolling – for the deliberate mailing of online abuse that *shouldn't* have been sent). But real letters, the kind with envelopes and stamps, have always felt – and still feel – more significant: you invest time and effort into putting your thoughts on paper, which makes the act of *not* sending them equally significant, especially as they are often written in times of acute crisis or emotional dilemma.

So in the process this became a book about human nature and motivation – about *why* a letter wasn't sent, and the extent to which *not* doing something can sometimes be as positive an act as doing it. The decision not to send a letter tells us a lot about ourselves, whether it's reached out of cowardice, or from an innate sense of caution, or even because we're far-sighted enough to realise the potential consequences.

The letters I tracked down – with the help of my publisher, Graham Coster, as well as the many friends and contacts who suggested potential leads to follow – were left unsent (or in some cases treated as *though* unsent) for all sorts of reasons, and with all sorts of consequences. Most are printed here complete with their original – often unorthodox – spelling and punctuation; some include the editorial interpretation with which they were first published. It wasn't always easy to decide which category a letter belonged in, and of course my musings are purely my own, but it's been fun to speculate.

The search took us through history and literature, biographies and journals; from world events to personal stories of caution, confusion and fatal indecision. There's JFK's subtle manoeuvring to avert a nuclear war, and Boris Johnson carelessly sabotaging his own bid for the Tory leadership. There are nearly-resignations by kings and politicians that might have altered history, and Virginia Woolf restraining herself from sending a particularly high-handed letter to the *New Statesman*. There's the letter from a girl to her sweetheart, injured on the Western Front, who died before she had a chance to post it; and the one *from* an officer at the Front, still unsent in his pocket when he was killed. And, from fiction, there's the love letter that gets left in a bar, unsent after a day's drinking, so that it's another 11 years before the couple finally get together.

Some were written out of an alcoholic haze, others bashed out by writers too hot-tempered to check either the sense or the spelling. The hazards include some Emily Dickinson hadn't even thought of – such as letters being misdirected, intercepted, read by the wrong person, or at the wrong time – making them perfect material for fiction: plays and novels are stuffed with correspondence whose progress doesn't quite go according to plan.

They range from the absurd to the almost unintelligible, and from the poignant to the unbearably sad. But they're all, somehow, a little more eloquent for being unsent.

Caroline Atkins
London
July 2018

I

Love Left Unsaid

There's a heart-stopping moment in *Marking Time*, the second book in Elizabeth Jane Howard's semi-autobiographical Cazalet chronicles, where 16-year-old Clary Cazalet receives a letter from her father Rupert, missing in wartime France for the last 18 months. Clary already treasures a postcard from her mother, who died when she was small ('Darling Clary . . . here's a picture of where Daddy and I are staying . . . Love from Mummy'), sent before Clary was even old enough to read it. 'For years afterwards,' says the author, 'she had lived on that love sent.' Now a pencilled note is delivered by hand, rather than posted, by specific instruction from Rupert, who understands the importance of it reaching her safely ('Not to post, to come myself', says the messenger). 'Darling Clary, I think of you every day. Love Dad.'

To Clary, it's all that needs to be said. 'The second piece of paper! The second piece of love sent!' Even with no way of knowing if Rupert is still alive, his words just have the poignancy of simple truth. (Elizabeth Jane Howard seems to have felt the need for authenticity in love, despite – or perhaps because of – her own multiple affairs and infidelities, and her involvement in her 70s with an admirer who turned out to be a liar and a conman. Embarking on her relationship with fellow writer Kingsley Amis in 1963, when she was 40 and they were both married to other people, she wrote to him, 'I love you more than I have loved anyone else. Had to wait to be sure it was true. It is.')

Think of those letters to Clary unsent, the love withheld, the feelings unspoken. Imagine the end of *Persuasion* without the letter that Captain Wentworth manages to write to Anne Elliot – while in the same room as her, and amid a whole party of chattering people, and while apparently at work on an entirely different document. Having hidden it under other papers on the table, at the last moment he draws it out and places it in front of her 'with eyes of glowing entreaty' before leaving the room. It is Wentworth's only way of addressing the woman who had been persuaded by her family to break off their engagement nearly a decade earlier, and whose affections – in Jane Austen's age of densely coded social signals – he is now unsure of: a spontaneous response to a half-overheard conversation that suggests she might still love him. 'I had not waited even these ten days, could I have read your feelings. . . I can hardly write. . .' It's a desperate plea for communication, for acknowledgment: 'I must speak to you by such means as are within my reach . . . I am half agony, half hope. Tell me not that I am too late . . .' And the killer line, overturning all doubt: 'I offer myself to you again with a heart even more your own, than when you almost broke it eight and a half years ago.' All that, and in a letter so nearly *not* sent. He cuts it breathtakingly fine.

Love letters are tangible proof that we once cared, and were cared for. We hoard them like holy relics, re-read them for reassurance, treasure them often for far longer than we should (sometimes long after the love itself has died), because to destroy them is to erase our own history.

Writing a love letter is an act of giving, a statement of feeling that, once sent, can't be taken back. And where emails and texts may have an instant-gratification immediacy, they are nothing to the anticipation of waiting for the post, recognising a lover's handwriting, slitting open the envelope . . . From that simple written *proof* of love, to the feelings too deeply held to speak aloud, the expression of love in letter form recurs throughout romantic novels, Shakespeare's plays and countless song lyrics. They may be written in the sand and destined to be obliterated by the tide (as declared by everyone from Andy Williams to Patsy Cline), they may be a petition, or a plea, or even a kind of prayer (according to Nick Cave), and they almost certainly come straight from your heart (Alison Moyet, Etta James, Tony Bennett et al).

That idea of wanting your love to be heard is irresistible. It's why, beneath the jaunty rhythm, Elvis Presley's 'Return to Sender' has the melancholy cry of a lover prevented from getting the words across. The letter he gives to the postman comes straight back the next day, and written on it is a message to the effect that there's no such house number, and indeed no such zone. Not just undelivered, then, but sent back *by* the woman he loves, a pointed rejection from the object of his affections.

So why, having written a love letter, would you not send it?

The reasons can range from confusion and uncertainty (Am I mad? What will he/she think of me?) to alcohol (in at least two cases quoted here) to bad timing and 'events' (even, in the saddest circumstances, the death of the writer or the recipient before the letter had a chance to be sent). Servicemen and women preparing to go into action routinely write letters to their families to be opened *if* they don't make it home. A friend of mine still has the sealed envelopes addressed to 'My wife', 'My son' and 'My daughter', that her husband wrote as an RAF officer: he's now back with them and no longer serving, but his unsent love is still there, locked safely away.

Perhaps, in some cases, we realise the letter isn't a genuine gift: we've composed it in an attempt to convince ourselves of love, or for our own selfish relief when our hearts are too full for comfort or sanity. Or perhaps we just accept that there's no point in sending it, that our love isn't – and won't ever be – reciprocated.

When the French-Scottish composer Erik Satie (of Gymnopédies fame) died in 1925, friends clearing out his apartment found scores of letters to Suzanne Valadon (muse and model to the Impressionists, mother of artist Maurice Utrillo and herself a gifted painter), with whom he'd had a six-month affair 30 years earlier, all written since she left him, and none of them sent. Weirdly, Satie was a devotee of the postal service (in the days when Paris had up to six deliveries a day, he would treat it like a memo board and send letters to *himself* as a reminder of important dates and events), but he had never mailed these – presumably realising his devotion was hopeless. She had married within a couple of years of ending their affair, and by the time he died she had divorced her first husband and was married again, to the painter Paul Utter (a friend of her son's and 20 years her junior).

Satie's brother Conrad delivered the letters by hand to Suzanne, who read them – and then burned them all. In one letter that does still exist, from March 1893, he rhapsodises about her 'lovely eyes', 'gentle hands' and 'tiny feet', and says that the thought of not seeing her that day fills him with an 'icy loneliness which makes my head go empty and fills my heart with sadness'. If that was when they were still together, what desperate yearning must there have been in those letters he never sent, in the years when she was no longer there for him.

Here are some of the most heartfelt expressions of love – in both life and literature – and it's just so sad to think of them not being sent.

Drunk but happy

Dexter to Emma in David Nicholls' *One Day*

It's amazing how quickly email has overtaken letters, odd how only relatively recently someone might have written a rambling, drunken letter and forgotten to post it, rather than writing a rambling drunken email and sending it by mistake. In David Nicholls' 2009 bestseller *One Day* – a novel where accidents of timing and alcohol-induced misunderstandings are key to the plot – Dexter Mayhew writes a gloriously beer-fuddled rant from the other side of the world to Emma Morley, the university friend with whom he had a one-night stand on graduation day.

It's two years later to the day – St Swithin's Day – and their lives have gone in different directions. Emma is serious, Northern, high-minded and idealistic: she dreams of living fully and well, staying true to her principles. She took their night together seriously, hoping it would lead somewhere; Dexter was already thinking, by the morning after, 'This must never, ever happen again'. He's Home Counties, arrogant and careless, already jaded and cynical at 23 or 24: he'd rather move on to another girl than face the disappointment of this one (or her disappointment with him, as he envisages it, at some future date). Since that graduation day encounter, the relationship Emma would have liked has settled into pen-friendship from their contrasting worlds: hers a series of badly paid jobs in dreary parts of the UK, his an extended gap-year tour of exotic destinations and easy lays. She writes him long intense letters of 'forced banter and barely concealed longing'; he sends brief shouty postcards that don't really convey any sense that he might be missing her. ('She would slip the postcards into the pocket of a heavy coat on long soulful walks on Ilkley Moor, searching for some hidden meaning in "VENICE COMPLETELY FLOODED!!!!".') Until she recognises that 'Letters, like compilation tapes, were really vehicles for unexpressed emotions and she was clearly putting far too much time and energy into them.'

Then, at precisely the same moment that Emma is working the Sunday lunchtime shift waitressing at a Mexican restaurant in Camden Town, Dexter – backpacking around India – writes this letter: drunkenly honest, openly vulnerable and for the first time admitting that their friendship might disguise something deeper.

Sunday 15th July 1990

Emma, Emma, Emma. How are you, Emma? And what are you doing right this second? We're six hours ahead here in Bombay, so hopefully you're still in bed with a Sunday morning hangover in which case WAKE UP! IT'S DEXTER!

This letter comes to you from a downtown Bombay hostel with scary mattresses and hot and cold running Australians. My guide book tells me that it has character i.e. rodents but my room also has a little plastic picnic table by the window and it's raining like crazy outside, harder even than in Edinburgh. It's CHUCKING IT DOWN, Em, so loud that I can barely hear the compilation tape you made me which I like a lot incidentally except for that jangly indie stuff because after all I'm not some GIRL. I've been trying to read the books you gave me at Easter too, though I have to admit I'm finding *Howards End* quite heavy-going. It's like they've been drinking the same cup of tea for two hundred pages, and I keep waiting for someone to pull a knife or an alien invasion or something, but that's not going to happen is it? When will you stop trying to educate me, I wonder? Never I hope.

By the way, in case you hadn't guessed from the Exquisite Prose and all the SHOUTING I'm writing this drunk, beers at lunchtime! As you can tell I'm not a great letter writer not like you (your last letter was so funny) but all I will say is that India is incredible. It turns out that being banned from Teaching English as a Foreign Language was the best thing that ever happened to me (though I still think they over-reacted. Morally Unfit? Me? Tove was twenty-one). I won't bore you with all that sunrise over the Hindu-kesh prose except to say that all the clichés are true (poverty, tummy upsets blah blah blah). Not only is it a rich and ancient civilization but you wouldn't BELIEVE what you can get in the chemists without a prescription.

So I've seen some amazing things and while it's not always fun it is an Experience and I've taken thousands of photographs which I will show you very very slooooooowly when I get back. Pretend to be interested, won't you? After all I pretended to be interested when you banged on about the Poll Tax riots. Anyway, I showed some of my photos to this TV producer who I met on a train the other day, a woman (not what you think, old, mid-thirties) and she said I could be a professional. She was here producing a sort of young people's TV travel show thing and she gave me her card and told me to call her in August when they're back again, so who knows maybe I'll do some researching or filming even.

What's happening with you work-wise? Are you doing another play? I really, really enjoyed your Virginia-Woolf-Emily-whatsername play when I was in London, and like I said I think it showed loads of promise which sounds like bullshit but isn't. I think you're right to give up acting though, not because you're not good but because you so obviously hate it. Candy was nice too, much nicer than you made out. Send her my love. Are you doing another play? Are you still in that box room? Does the flat still smell of fried onions? Is Tilly Killick still soaking her big grey bras in the washing-up bowl? Are you still at Mucho Loco or whatever it's called? Your last letter made me laugh so much, Em, but you should still get out of there because while it's good for gags it's definitely bad for your soul. You can't throw years of your life away because it makes a funny anecdote.

Which brings me to my reason for writing to you. Are you ready? You might want to sit down . . .

Since I started this letter I've drank (drunken? dronk?) two more beers and so am ready to say this now. Here goes. Em, we've known each other five or six years now, but two years properly, as, you know, 'friends', which isn't that long but I think I know a bit about you and I think I know what your problem is. And be aware that I have a lowish 2.2 in Anthropology, so I know what I'm talking about. If you don't want to know my theory, stop reading now.

Good. Here is it. I think you're scared of being happy, Emma. I think you think that the natural way of things is for your life to be grim and grey and dour and to hate your job, hate where you live, not to have success or money or God forbid a boyfriend (and a quick discersion here – that whole self-deprecating thing about being unattractive is getting pretty boring I can tell you). In fact I'll go further and say that I think you actually get a kick out of being disappointed and under-achieving, because it's easier, isn't it? Failure and unhappiness is easier because you can make a joke out of it. Is this annoying you? I bet it is. Well I've only just started.

Em, I hate thinking of you sitting in that awful flat with the weird smells and noises and the overhead lightbulbs or sat in that launderette, and by the way there's no reason in this day and age why you should be using a launderette, there's nothing cool or political about launderettes it's just depressing. I don't know, Em, you're young, you're practically a genius, and yet your idea of a good time is to treat yourself to a service wash. Well I think you deserve more. You are smart and funny and kind (too kind if you ask me) and by far the cleverest person I know. And (am drinking more beer here – deep breath) you are also a Very Attractive Woman. And (more beer) yes I do mean 'sexy' as well, though I feel a bit sick writing it down. Well I'm not going to scribble it out because it's politically incorrect to call someone 'sexy' because it is also TRUE. You're gorgeous, you old hag, and if I could give you just one gift ever for the rest of your life it would be this. Confidence. It would be the gift of Confidence. Either that or a scented candle.

I know from your letters and from seeing you after your play that you feel a little bit lost right now about what to do with your life, a bit rudderless and oarless and aimless but that's okay that's alright because we're all meant to be like that at twenty-four. In fact our whole generation is like that. I read an article about it, it's because we never fought in a war or watched too much television or something. Anyway, the only people with oars and rudders and aims are dreary bores and squares and careerists like Tilly-bloody-Killick or Callum O'Neill and his refurbished computers. I certainly don't have a master plan I know you think I've got it all sorted out but I haven't I worry too I just don't worry about the dole and housing benefit and the future of the Labour Party and where I'm going to be in twenty years' time and how Mr Mandela is adjusting to freedom.

So time for another breather before the next paragraph because I've barely got started. This letter builds to a life-changing climax. I wonder if you're ready for it yet.

The thing is, Em, running back to the hostel in the rain just now – the rain is warm here, hot even sometimes, not like London rain – I was, like I said, pretty drunk and I found myself thinking about you and thinking what a shame Em isn't here to see this, to experience this, and I had this revelation and it's this.

You should be here with me. In India.

And this is my big idea, and it might be insane, but

I'm going to post this before I change my mind. Follow these simple instructions.

1 – Leave that crappy job right now. Let them find someone else to melt cheese on tortilla chips for 2.20 an hour. Put a bottle of tequila in your bag and walk out the door. Think what that will feel like, Em. Walk out now, Just do it.

2 – I also think you should leave that flat. Tilly's ripping you off, charging all that money for a room without a window. It isn't a box room, it's a box, and you should get out of there and let someone else wring out her great big grey bras for her. When I get back to the so-called real world I'm going to buy a flat because that's the kind of over-privileged capitalist monster I am and you're always welcome to come and stay for a bit, or permanently if you like, because I think we'd get on, don't you? As, you know, FLATMATES. That's providing you can overcome your sexual attraction to me ha ha. If the worst comes to the worst, I'll lock you in your room at nights. Anyway, now the big one –

3 – As soon as you've read this, go to the student travel agency on Tottenham Court Road and book an OPEN RETURN flight to Delhi to arrive as near as possible to August 1st, two weeks' time, which in case you've forgotten is my birthday. The night before get a train to Agra and stay in a cheap motel. Next morning get up early and go to the Taj Mahal. Perhaps you've heard of it, big white building named after that Indian restaurant on the Lothian Road. Have a look around and at precisely 12 midday you stand directly under the centre of the dome with a red rose in one hand and a

copy of *Nicholas Nickleby* in the other and I will come and find you, Em. I will be carrying a white rose and my copy of *Howards End* and when I see you I will throw it at your head.

Isn't that the greatest plan you've ever heard of in your life?

Ah, typical Dexter you say, isn't he forgetting something? Money! Plane tickets don't grow on trees and what about social security and the work ethic etc. etc. Well don't worry, I'm paying. Yes, I'm paying. I'm going to wire the money to you for your plane ticket (I've always wanted to wire money) and I'm going to pay for everything when you're here which sounds swanky but isn't because it is so DAMN CHEAP here. We can live for months, Em, me and you, heading down to Kerala or across to Thailand. We could go to a full moon party – imagine staying awake all night not because you're worried about the future but because it's FUN. (Remember when we stayed up all night after graduation, Em? Anyway. Moving on.)

For three hundred pounds of someone else's money, you could change your life, and you mustn't worry about it because frankly I have money that I haven't earned, and you work really hard and yet you don't have money, so it's socialism in action isn't it? And if you really want you can pay me back when you're a famous playwright, or when the poetry-money kicks in or whatever. Besides it's only for three months. I've got to come back in the autumn anyway. As you know Mum's not been well. She tells me the operation went fine and maybe it did or maybe she just doesn't want me to worry. Either way I've got to come home eventually. (By the way, my mother has a theory about you and me, and if you meet me at the Taj Mahal I will tell you all about it, but only if you meet me.)

On the wall in front of me is this massive sort of praying mantis thing and he's looking at me as if to say shut up now so I will. It's stopped raining, and I'm about to go to a bar and meet up with some new friends for a drink, three female medical students from Amsterdam which tells you all you need to know. But on the way I'm going to find a post box and send this before I change my mind. Not because I think you coming here is a bad idea – it isn't, it's a great idea and you must come – but because I think I may have said too much. Sorry if this has annoyed you. The main thing is that I think about you a lot, that's all. Dex and Em, Em and Dex. Call me sentimental, but there's no-one in the world that I'd like to see get dysentery more than you.

Taj Mahal, 1st August, 12 noon.

I will find you!

Love

D

Re-reading it sober, Dexter is beset by last-minute doubts but – presumably convinced by the sheer candour of that line about dysentery – decides to send it anyway, tucking the letter inside Emma's copy of *Howards End* when he heads out to meet his new friends. (It's surely not a coincidence that David Nicholls gave Dexter this particular novel to put in his rucksack, as it's another story that turns on letters sent and unsent – see Chapter VI. Emma, of course, represents the Schlegels, trying to introduce him, like the Wilcoxes, to culture.)

Later in the evening, after Dexter has left the crowded bar in the company of another conquest, the book and the letter are found, slipped down between the scruffy sofa cushions, by a German student, who reads it and considers it 'not quite a love letter, but near enough' to be worth receiving by this Emma Morley, whoever she is. With no address to send it to, however, she ends up taking it with her – and 18 years later the book is on a shelf in her Frankfurt spare room, with the letter still inside it.

It's juvenile, ill-spelt, ungrammatical and clumsy – but it *is* a love letter in its own way, and Dexter is probably being more true to himself here than he manages to be in another 300-odd pages. And if he had only remembered to post it, that might have been the end of the book: we know they're meant to be together, and the drunker he gets, the more surely he feels it too. Instead, there are 11 more St Swithin's Days to go . . .

Drunk and desperate

The Consul to Yvonne, in Malcolm Lowry's *Under the Volcano*

Like Dexter in *One Day*, Geoffrey Firmin writes his love letter under the influence of alcohol (mescal, this time, rather more potent than beer). This is another novel constructed around the events of a single day – but whereas *One Day* revisits the same date over 20 years, *Under the Volcano*, set in the shadow of Popocatepetl and Ixtaccihuatl, recounts the final hours in the life of one man, Geoffrey Firmin, former British Consul, on Mexico's Day of the Dead in 1938. And the Consul's letter – written to his ex-wife, Yvonne (who had left him *because* of his drinking), and begging her to come back to him – remains unread until much later, when it is discovered (again inside a book, this one of Elizabethan plays) by his old friend Jacques Laruelle (who had himself had an affair with Yvonne).

This is a desperate plea rather than alcohol-fuelled bravado. Dexter's relationship with Emma hadn't yet got underway, his love for her was still embryonic – but the Consul's is written after the end of his marriage, when the relationship has already gone wrong. He knows what he's lost, whereas Dexter seems to have no idea of how lucky he is even to have a chance with Emma. So in place of Dexter's colloquial teen-speak we get fiery, impassioned eloquence: 'Alas, what has happened to the love and understanding we once had! What is going to happen to it – what is going to happen to our hearts?' Where the beers mellowed Dexter, the mescal tips the Consul into a place of terrifying, hallucinatory visions and extraordinary energy (complete with a 348-word sentence in the fourth paragraph), interspersed with occasional moments of clarity such as, 'Love is the only thing which gives meaning to our poor ways on earth: not precisely a discovery, I am afraid.'

We realise that this is just one of many attempts to write to Yvonne ('trembling and sweltering in the post office and writing telegrams all afternoon, when I had drunk enough to steady my hand, without having sent one'). And the letter itself – the paper and the writing – is so clearly sketched that you can see the words as vividly as the images they evoke. It's on 'two sheets of uncommonly thin hotel notepaper that had been pressed flat in the book, long but narrow and crammed on both sides with meaningless writing in pencil . . . the hand half crabbed, half generous, and wholly drunken'. Laruelle recognises it as unmistakably the Consul's: 'the Greek e's, flying buttresses of d's, the t's like lonely wayside crosses save where they crucified the entire word, the words themselves slanting steeply downhill, though the individual characters seemed as if resisting the descent, braced, climbing the other way'. It's the writing of a tragic hero, torturing himself with his memories and dreams, and sinking into a hell of despair.

Hotel Bella Vista

. . . Night: and once again, the nightly grapple with death, the room shaking with daemonic orchestras, the snatches of fearful sleep, the voices outside the window, my name being continually repeated with scorn by imaginary parties arriving, the dark's spinnets. As if there were not enough real noises in these nights the colour of grey hair. Not like the rending tumult of American cities, the noise of the unbandaging of great giants in agony. But the howling pariah dogs, the cocks that herald dawn all night, the drumming, the moaning that will be found later white plumage huddled on telegraph wires in back gardens or fowl roosting in apple trees, the eternal sorrow that never sleeps of great Mexico. For myself I like to take my sorrow into the shadow of old monasteries, my guilt into cloisters and under tapestries, and into the misericordes of unimaginable *cantinas* where sad-faced potters and legless beggars drink at dawn, whose cold jonquil beauty one rediscovers in death. So that when you left, Yvonne, I went to Oaxaca. There is no sadder word. Shall I tell you, Yvonne, of the terrible journey there through the desert over the narrow gauge railway on the rack of a third-class carriage bench, the child whose life its mother and I saved by rubbing its belly with tequila out of my bottle, or of how, when I went to my room in the hotel where we once were happy, the noise of slaughtering below in the kitchen drove me out into the glare of the street, and later, that night, there was a vulture sitting in the washbasin? Horrors portioned to a giant nerve! No, my secrets are of the grave and must be kept. And this is how I sometimes think of myself, as a great explorer who has discovered some extraordinary land from which he can never return to give his knowledge to the world: but the name of this land is hell.

It is not Mexico of course but in the heart. And today I was in Quauhnahuac as usual when I received from my lawyers news of our divorce. This was as I invited it. I received other news too: England is breaking off diplomatic relations with Mexico and all her Consuls – those, that is, who are English – are being called home. These are kindly and good men, for the most part, whose name I suppose I demean. I shall not go home with them. I shall perhaps go home but not to England, not to that home. So, at midnight, I drove in the Plymouth to Tomalín to see my Tlaxcaltecan friend Cervantes the cockfighter at the Salón Ofélia. And thence I came to the Farolito in Parián where I sit now in a little room off the bar at four-thirty in the morning drinking *ochas* and then *mescal* and writing this on some Bella Vista notepaper I filched the other night, perhaps because the writing paper at the Consulate, which is a tomb, hurts me to look at. I think I know a good deal about physical suffering. But this is worst of all, to feel your soul dying. I wonder if it is because tonight my soul has really died that I feel at the moment something like peace.

Or is it because right through hell there is a path, as Blake well knew, and though I may not take it, sometimes lately in dreams I have been able to see it? And here is one strange effect my lawyer's news has had upon me. I seem to see now, between mescals, this path, and beyond it strange vistas, like visions of a new life together we might somewhere lead. I seem to see us living in some northern country, of mountains and hills and blue water; our house is built on an inlet and one evening we are standing, happy in one another, on the balcony of this house, looking over the water. There are sawmills half hidden by trees beyond and under the hills on the other side of the inlet, what looks like an oil refinery, only softened and rendered beautiful by distance.

It is a light blue moonless summer evening, but late, perhaps ten o'clock, with Venus burning hard in daylight, so we are certainly somewhere far north, and standing on this balcony, when from beyond along the coast comes the gathering thunder of a long many-engined freight train, thunder because although we are separated by this wide strip of water from it, the train is rolling eastward and the changing wind veers for the moment from an easterly quarter, and we face east, like Swedenborg's angels, under a sky clear save where far to the north-east over distant mountains whose purple has faded, lies a mass of almost pure white clouds, suddenly, as by light in an alabaster lamp, illumined from within by gold lightning, yet you can hear no thunder, only the roar of the great train with its engines and its wide shunting echoes as it advances from the hills into the mountains: and then all at once a fishing-boat with tall gear comes running round the point like a white giraffe, very swift and stately, leaving directly behind it a long silver scalloped rim of wake, not visibly moving inshore, but now stealing ponderously beachward towards us, this scrolled silver rim of wash striking the shore first in the distance, then spreading all along the curve of beach, its growing thunder and commotion now joined to the diminishing thunder of the train, and now breaking reboant on our beach, while the floats, for there are timber diving floats, are swayed together, everything jostled and beautifully ruffled and stirred and tormented in this rolling sleeked silver, then little by little calm again, and you see the reflection of the remote white thunderclouds in the water, and now the lightning within the white clouds in deep water, as the fishing-boat itself with a golden scroll of travelling light in its silver wake beside it reflected from the cabin vanishes round the headland, silence, and then again, within the white white distant alabaster thunderclouds beyond the mountains, the thunderless gold lightning in the blue evening, unearthly . . .

And as we stand looking all at once comes the wash of another unseen ship, like a great wheel, the vast spokes of the wheel whirling across the bay –

(Several mescals later.) Since December 1937, and you went, and it is now I hear the spring of 1938, I have been deliberately struggling against my love for you. I dared not submit to it. I have grasped at every root and branch which would help me across this abyss in my life by myself but I can deceive myself no longer. If I am to survive I need your help. Otherwise, sooner or later, I shall fall. Ah, if only you had given me something in memory to hate you for so finally no kind thought of you would ever touch me in this terrible place where I am! But instead you sent me those letters. Why did you send the first ones to Wells Fargo in Mexico City, by the way? Can it be you didn't realize I was still here? – Or – if in Oaxaca – that Quauhnahuac was still my base? That is very peculiar. It would have been so easy to find out too. And if you'd only written me *right away* also, it might have been different – sent me a postcard even, out of the common anguish of our separation, appealing simply to *us*, in spite of it all, to end the absurdity immediately – somehow, anyhow – and saying we loved each other, something, or a telegram, simple. But you waited too long – or so it seems now, till after Christmas – Christmas! – and the New Year, and then what you sent I couldn't read. No: I have scarcely been once free enough from torment or sufficiently sober to apprehend more than the governing design of any of these letters. But I could, can feel them. I think I have some of them on me. But they are too painful to read, they seem too long digested. I shall not attempt it now. I cannot read them. They break my heart. And they came too late anyway. And now I suppose there will be no more.

Alas, but why have I not pretended at least that I had read them, accepted some meed of retraction in the fact that they were sent? And why did I not send a telegram or some word immediately? Ah, why not, why not, why not? For I suppose you would have come back in due course if I had asked you? But this is what it is to live in hell. I could not, cannot ask you. I could not, cannot sent a telegram. I have stood here, and in Mexico City, in the Compañía Telegráfica Mexicana, and in Oaxaca, trembling and sweltering in the post office and writing telegrams all afternoon, when I had drunk enough to steady my hand, without having sent one. And once I had some number of yours and actually called you long distance to Los Angeles though without success. And another time the telephone broke down. Then why do I not come to America myself? I am too ill to arrange about the tickets, to suffer the shaking delirium of the endless weary cactus plains. And why go to America to die? Perhaps I would not mind being buried in the United States. But I think I would prefer to die in Mexico.

Meantime do you see me as still working on the book, still trying to answer such questions as: Is there any ultimate reality, external, conscious, and ever-present, etc. etc., that can be realized by any such means that may be acceptable to all creeds and religions and suitable to all climes and countries? Or do you find me between Mercy and Understanding, between Chesed and Binah (but still at Chesed) – my equilibrium, and equilibrium is all, precarious – balancing, teetering over the awful unbridgeable void, the all-but-unretraceable path of God's lightning back to God? as if I ever were in Chesed! More like the Qliphoth. When I should have been producing obscure volumes of verse entitled the Triumph of Humpty Dumpty or the Nose with the Luminous Dong! Or at best, like Clare, 'weaving fearful vision' . . . A frustrated poet in every man. Though it is perhaps a good idea under the circumstances to pretend at least to be proceeding with one's great work on 'Secret Knowledge', then one can always say when it never comes out that the title explains this deficiency.

But alas for the Knight of Sorry Aspect! For oh, Yvonne, I am so haunted continuously by the thought of your songs, of your warmth and merriment, of your simplicity and comradeship, of your abilities in a hundred ways, your fundamental sanity, your untidiness, your equally excessive neatness – the sweet beginnings of our marriage. Do you remember the Strauss song we used to sing? Once a year the dead live for one day. Oh come to me again as once in May. The Generalife Gardens and the Alhambra Gardens. And shadows of our fate at our meeting in Spain. The Hollywood bar in Granada. Why Hollywood? And the nunnery there: why Los Angeles? And in Malaga, the Pensión México. And yet nothing can ever take the place of the unity we once knew and which Christ alone knows must still exist somewhere. Knew even in Paris – before Hugh came. Is this an illusion too? I am being completely maudlin certainly. But no one can take your place; I ought to know by now, I laugh as I write this, whether I love you or not . . . Sometimes I am possessed by a most powerful feeling, a despairing bewildered jealousy which, when deepened by drink, turns into a desire to destroy myself by my own imagination – not at least to be the prey of – ghosts –

(Several mescalitos later and down in the Farolito). . . Time is a fake healer anyhow. How can anyone presume to tell me about you? You cannot know the sadness of my life. Endlessly haunted waking and sleeping by the thought that you may need my help, which I cannot give, as I need yours, which you cannot, seeing you in visions and in every shadow, I have been compelled to write this, which I shall never send, to ask you what we can do. Is not that extraordinary? And yet – do we not owe it ourselves, to that self we created, apart from us, to try again? Alas, what has happened to the love and understanding we once had! What is going to happen to it – what is going to happen to our hearts? Love is the only thing which gives meaning to our poor ways on earth: not precisely a discovery, I am afraid. You will think I am mad, but this is how I drink too, as if I were taking an eternal sacrament. Oh Yvonne, we cannot allow what we created to sink down to oblivion in this dingy fashion –

Lift up your eyes unto the hills, I seem to hear a voice saying. Sometimes, when I see the little red mail plane fly in from Acapulco at seven in the morning over the strange hills, or more probably hear, lying trembling, shaking, and dying in bed (when I am in bed at that time) – just a tiny roar and gone – as I reach out babbling for the glass of *mescal*, the drink that I can never believe even in raising to my lips is real, that I have had the marvellous foresight to put within easy reach the night before, I think that you will be on it, on that plane every morning as it goes by, and will have come to save me. Then the morning goes by and you have not come. But oh, I pray for this now, that you will come. On second thoughts I do not see why from Acapulco. But for God's sake, Yvonne, hear me, my defences are down, at the moment they are down – and there goes the plane, I heard it in the distance then, just for an instant, beyond Tomalín – come back, come back. I will stop drinking, anything. I am dying without you. For Christ Jesus' sake Yvonne come back to me, hear me, it is a cry, come back to me, Yvonne, if only for a day . . .

Which she does – or, rather, did. This unsent letter, which Laruelle burns after reading, takes him back to events of a year earlier, when Yvonne did come back, to challenge the Consul over his drinking. The rest of the book is told in flashback over that day, and in the final chapter we realise that Yvonne had been writing her own desperate unanswered letters to the Consul, none of which he received.

It's a complex, visionary novel that echoes Lowry's own tormented imagination, and has a strong autobiographical element. He himself lived in Mexico on and off for a decade, and his first wife, Jan Gabrial, left him several times because of his drinking. He spent nearly ten years writing and revising the book (which partly accounts for its notorious, multi-layered complexity – it would probably take almost as long to understand it). It began as a short story in 1936, when he was married to Jan, is set during 1938 (the year that marriage broke up), was revised from 1940 and 1944 (with editorial help from his second wife, Margerie Bonner), and was nearly lost in a fire at their beach house in British Columbia (he lost at least one other novel that way) before finally being published in 1947.

As for his own letters, he was often too drunk, distressed or lost in his ideas to finish them. 'I have tried ten times to write this letter and have not yet succeeded,' he wrote to one friend in 1954. On another occasion, in 1955, Margerie wrote to his editor: 'Malc had been trying to write you for two weeks, but the letter became more and more involved, longer, and in trying to say something, poor soul, he ended by saying nothing comprehensible, so I'm trying to figure out what he really meant to say, and say it for him.'

Fortunately, one letter he did complete – and send – was to his publisher, Jonathan Cape, who had suggested even more revisions to the manuscript of *Under the Volcano*. Lowry wrote him a 40-page response of such conviction (it's generally taken to be the most remarkable critical analysis by an author of his own work) that Cape was persuaded to backtrack and publish the book without changing a word.

The last post

Captain Scott's final letter to his wife

The story of Captain Robert Falcon Scott's expedition to the South Pole is a classic tale of British grit, heroism and sacrifice. He and his team reached their destination on 17 January 1912, after trekking more than 850 miles across glaciers and ice fields, only to find that the Norwegian explorer Roald Amundsen had beaten them to it. And having failed in their mission to get there first, they then failed to make it back to their base camp. Scott and his two remaining companions (two others had died a week earlier, Oates famously 'just going outside' into the blizzard and not coming back) gave up within three days of their nearest food depot, and their frozen bodies weren't discovered until November. It's not known exactly when he died, although the final entry in his journal is dated 29 March 1912: 'It seems a pity,' he says, 'but I do not think I can write more. R. Scott.' And there's a final request: 'For God's sake look after our people.' But actually, his farewell letter to his wife Kathleen, found with his journal, shows that he had faith in her to look after herself.

It isn't entirely a love letter, partly because he's determined not to let sentimentality make it even more upsetting for Kathleen, and partly because he has practical things he wants to say. He knows that he will be dead by the time she reads it, so as well as his own grief at the thought of never seeing his wife and son again, he's got their future to think of. Most of all, he wants to reassure her.

To my widow,

Dearest Darling – we are in a very tight corner and I have doubts of pulling through – In our short lunch hours I take advantage of a very small measure of warmth to write letters preparatory to a possible end – the first is naturally to you on whom my thoughts mostly dwell waking or sleeping – if anything happens to me I shall like you to know how much you have meant to me and that pleasant recollections are with me as I depart.

I should like you to take what comfort you can from these facts also – I shall not have suffered any pain but leave the world fresh from harness and full of good health and vigour – this is dictated already, when provisions come to an end we simply stop where we are within easy distance of another depot.

Therefore you must not imagine a great tragedy – we are very anxious of course and have been for weeks but in splendid physical condition and our appetites compensate for all discomfort. The cold is biting and sometimes angering but here again the hot food which drives it forth is so wonderfully enjoyable that we would scarcely be without it.

We have gone down hill a good deal since I wrote the above. Poor Titus Oates has gone – he was in a bad state – the rest of us keep going and imagine we have a chance to get through but the cold weather doesn't let up at all

– we are now only 20 miles from a depot but we have very little food or fuel.

Well dear heart I want you to take the whole thing very sensibly as I am sure you will – the boy will be your comfort. I had looked forward to helping you to bring him up but it is a satisfaction to feel that he is safe with you. I think both he and you ought to be specially looked after by the country for which after all we have given our lives with something of spirit which makes for example – I am writing letters on this point in the end of this book after this. Will you send them to their various destinations?

I must write a little letter for the boy if time can be found to be read when he grows up – dearest heart, you know I cherish no sentimental rubbish about re marriage – when the right man comes to help you in life you ought to be your happy self again.

I wasn't a very good husband but I hope I shall be a good memory certainly the end is nothing for you to be ashamed of and I like to think that the boy will have a good start in parentage of which he may be proud. Dear it is not easy to write because of the cold – 70 degrees below zero and nothing but the shelter of our tent.

You know I have loved you, you know my thoughts must have constantly dwelt on you and oh dear me you must know that quite the worst aspect of this situation is the thought that I shall not see you again. The inevitable must be faced – you urged me to be leader of this party and I know you felt it would be dangerous – I've taken my place throughout, haven't I?

God bless you my own darling I shall try and write more later – I go on across the back pages. Since writing the above we have got to within 11 miles of our depot with one hot meal and two days cold food and we should have got through but have been held for four days by a frightful storm – I think the best chance has gone. We have decided not to kill ourselves but to fight it to the last for that depot but in the fighting there is a painless end so don't worry.

I have written letters on odd pages of this book – will you manage to get them sent? You see I am anxious for you and the boy's future – make the boy interested in natural history if you can, it is better than games – they encourage it at some schools – I know you will keep him out in the open air – try and make him believe in a God, it is comforting.

Oh my dear my dear what dreams I have had of his future and yet oh my girl I know you will face it stoically – your portrait and the boy's will be found in my breast and the one in the little red Morocco case given by Lady Baxter. There is a piece of the Union flag I put up at the South Pole in my private kit bag together with Amundsen's black flag and other trifles – give a small piece of the Union flag to the King and a small piece to Queen Alexandra and keep the rest a poor trophy for you!

What lots and lots I could tell you of this journey. How much better it has been than lounging in comfort at home – what tales you would have for the boy but oh what a price to pay – to forfeit the sight of your dear dear face.

> Dear you will be good to the old mother. I write her a little line in this book. Also keep in with Ettie and the others – oh but you'll put on a strong face for the world – only don't be too proud to accept help for the boy's sake – he ought to have a fine career and do something in the world.
>
> I haven't time to write to Sir Clements [Sir Clements Markham, president of the Royal Geographical Society, had put Scott in charge of the RRS *Discovery* expedition to Antarctica 10 years earlier] – tell him I thought much of him and never regretted him putting me in command of the *Discovery* – Give messages of farewell to Lady Baxter and Lady Sandhurst keep friends with them for both are dear women & to also both the Reginald Smiths

The letter is left unfinished and unsigned – he just stops writing, in the middle of these last-minute messages and reminders to Kathleen.

It's the stoical, mustn't-grumble Britishness that gets you, the lack of melodrama or self-pity, as though he's stuck on a train and won't make it home in time for the school parents' evening. The address, 'To my widow', sums up the bleakness of his position. Yet instead of despair or fear, we get that wistful line about 'What lots and lots I could tell you of this journey' – the sense that his greatest loss is not being able to share his stories with them, that by going on this adventure he has forfeited his future with her, at only 46. So the tone slips between genuine distress at the thought of not seeing her again and pragmatic coaching in best management style – expressing his confidence in her ability to cope and 'take it sensibly'.

Which she clearly did: Kathleen Scott (née Kennet) was a remarkable woman. A sculptor in her own right, she had been befriended by Auguste Rodin (who also introduced her to Isadora Duncan) while at art school in Paris, and later became acquainted with writers including George Bernard Shaw, Max Beerbohm and J. M. Barrie. She followed Scott's advice about finding a new husband, marrying politician Edward Hilton Young ten years after his death. And perhaps the most striking comment is his plea for her to 'make the boy interested in nature' – an inspired piece of posthumous career advice, given that the boy grew up to be the world-renowned ornithologist and conservationist Peter Scott.

Interestingly, unsent letters seem to be a recurring features of the Scott family. Peter was only nine months old when the expedition set off in 1910, so he had no memories of his famous father. But after his mother's death in 1947, he found a letter she herself had written to him in 1923 (when he was 14), and never sent, just before the birth of his half-brother which she thought she might not survive (she was 45, which she describes to her son as 'getting fairly old'). Like her husband, she wanted him not to be too miserable in the event of her death, and to remember that she would always be cheering for him. Maybe she was thinking about how helpful it was having her husband's letter to sustain her. And maybe she was talking from personal experience when she told him that any sadness he might feel would pass 'surprisingly soon':

> Little sweetheart: I want the person who tells you that I am dead to give you this letter. I am writing it before I die, because I am afraid I may. I want you to take it very sensibly. Don't be too miserable. I've had a *lovely* life, but I'm getting fairly old and it's very nice (since one must die sometime) to do so before one gets ill and blind and deaf and bored and tiresome. So let's all be quite cheerful

about it. And remember that *if* I can see you in any way after I'm dead (though I don't think one can, but one can't be too sure) I shall want to see you gay and merry and funny – working hard and playing and keeping Hilton happy. No tears for me dearie! Only hurray, that your gay little mother stayed happy till she died.

I'm not going to give you lots of good advice, only this: 'Keep fit!' and I've taught you how to do this. I wouldn't learn to smoke or drink if I were you, but if you do, be moderate. Add to that 'Be always kind', and with those two precepts you should be happy. If you feel sadly about me now, know that it will pass surprisingly soon. I shall not be unhappy, so you must not be. If you feel inclined to howl, go out and run violently and know that I am shouting 'Bravo' to you. Bless you ever.

Peter himself ended up married to the novelist Elizabeth Jane Howard for nine years (a couple of decades before she met Kingsley Amis), and in July 1946, when their marriage was breaking down, he wrote her an unsent love letter of his own from Slimbridge in Gloucestershire, where he was setting up his first nature reserve.

Darling darling Jenny . . .

It is very *peaceful* here. I have just walked out on to the bridge over the canal, and along the banks were a dozen or more little twinkling stars amongst the grass. Glow-worms. I walked along the bank amongst them and bent down to watch them crawling up the grass stems, lit by the light of their own green halo. Is it all right to mention them? – they aren't really worms at all, but the

> caterpillars of a beetle and they look like this [drawing], and the light shines from under their tails. It is amazingly bright. As I walked back and over the bridge and looked at them from across the canal I could still see the light from one of them at 100 yards . . . My decoy is incredibly beautiful, with the tall willows silver grey in their full leaf. It is a lovely place and I am pleased to have it . . . I'm afraid it will not please you at all if I tell you how much I love you. *Embarras de richesse* – everyone loves you and why wouldn't they – poor things.

By this time, Peter was spending most of his weekends at Slimbridge, while his wife (generally known as Jane) stayed in their London house and conducted an intense but not very happy affair with a literary agent and narrow-boat enthusiast called Robert Aickman.

Peter still adored Jane, and the letter is beautiful and eloquent - but might it give some clue to the problems in their marriage that even in a love letter he talks mostly about wildlife? That query about mentioning the worms: the Scotts had only recently shared their cabin with an assortment of snakes on a crossing from New York, so she clearly had no physical problem with them - but was he perhaps aware that talking about them would irritate her? He knew Jane had felt increasingly isolated from his interests - as well as overshadowed by the formidable Kathleen, now her mother-in-law, who was ultra-possessive of her son.

His declaration at the end seems terribly sad and tentative in the way it anticipates her displeasure, and her loveableness somehow comes across as an empirical fact that he knows to be true, rather than something he feels. Is that, perhaps, why the letter remained unsent?

Love remembered

Patrick Leigh Fermor to Marie-Blanche Cantacuzène

This one probably belongs in the 'Thought Better Of' category, but it's written as a love letter, so let's give him the benefit of the doubt. Travel writer, war hero and incurable romantic Patrick Leigh Fermor had been in love with Marie-Blanche Cantacuzène ten years earlier, and had spent almost five years with her before the start of the Second World War. His first love, she was more than ten years older than him, a Rumanian princess married to a Spanish diplomat who had left her for another woman. By 1946 he hadn't seen her for seven years and was already in love with Joan Rayner (whom he eventually married in 1968), but was still in touch with Balasha, as she was known, so this letter was a reply to one of hers.

Written from Greece, where they had spent two summers together, it starts by reminiscing about favourite places and old friends, but then lapses increasingly into travel-journalism mode, complete with evocative descriptions of darting fish and silver olive groves. Somehow when he talks of people they both knew – 'Yorgo with awkward hands resting on the shaft of his crook, Stamatina's pretty wrinkled face smiling out of its black headdress' – these feel like opportunities to add local colour, rather than a genuine memory-prompt to Balasha: why give such rich detail to someone who already knows the picture? Even when he recalls her presence there, it reads as though he's re-creating her for a wider audience, like a character in a story, with her 'grey wool Athens suit, silk shirt, blue-and-white tie, and small round white hat' – and for all the darlings and hugs and kisses, you slightly doubt the authenticity of feeling.

To Balasha Cantacuzène*

Easter Saturday 1946 Poros

My own darling,

The clock has suddenly slipped back ten years, and here I am sitting in front of our café in the small square, at a green-topped iron table on one of those rickety chairs. The marble-lantern, with its marine symbols – anchors and dolphins – is within reach of my arm; the drooping tree has been cut down. But the same old men, in broad shady hats, snowy *fustanellas* [skirt-like garments traditionally worn by men in southern Europe] and moustaches, sit conversing quietly over their *narghiléhs* [shisha pipes]. They all bowed and greeted me warmly, but soberly as if I had seen them only yesterday; my hand still aches from the iron grasp of Christo, the smiling Mongolian *kafedzi* [café-proprietor] – 'Where's Kyria Balasha? How is she?' they all cry. – Mitso the boatman, Spiro's *coumbáros* [god-brother] at the grocer's shop, the man at the zachaaro-plasteion [shop selling sweet cakes], the barber, the chaps in the little walled restaurant, and a dozen whiskered friends – especially Tomás, the one armed forest-guard, all down here for the Easter

* This letter is reproduced from the published edition of Patrick Leigh Fermor's letters, *Dashing for the Post*, complete with all the editor's parenthetical glosses and translations.

ceremonies. Loud shrieks of delight from Uncle Alcibiades's daughter, married now. Best of all, three tall young men – guess who? Niko, Yanni and Andrea, and a strapping Tasso in his teens. Spiro is up at the mill, with 13-year-old Kosta and Katrina, and, isn't it amazing?, ten-years-old Evtychia! Devout Marina is across the water at Galata, busy at her religious observances. Stop! Who do you think has just come and sat at my table, flinging an affectionate arm round my shoulders? Yanni, our boatman, who taught us the names of the winds, and always rowed us to Plaka. His brother Mitso told him I was here. He is a sailor now, veteran of countless battles, and as charming and gay and simple as ever and sends heaps of love to you."E!'Η Μπαλάσσα! 'Η Μπαλάσσα! Τι καλή γυναίκα! ['E! Ah! Balsha! Balasha! What a nice lady!'] They all adore us both here, and are real friends.

I arrived last night, and have not been to the hill yet. I am going today with Yanni and tomorrow for Easter Sunday, where Spiro is going to roast a huge lamb, and all our friends will assemble from the lemon-forest to eat it. I'll take a camera with me, and send you lots of photographs.

A caïque brought me here – the *Hydra*, the *Pteroti*, and *Avli* were sunk by the Germans – and it was very beautiful. I missed you dreadfully, Balasha darling, as we slid over those silk-smooth waters between dreaming islands: the same soft air caressed our ams and hands and temples, the same light wind carried the smell of pine-needles and thyme to one's nostrils, and I had the same argonaut plus conquistador feeling of being the first traveller to cross these ancient waters and gulfs and lagoons. The moment the caïque anchored at the quay, I jumped ashore, and walked to the monastery, along that lovely road winding under the pines overhanging the steep timbered cliffs, and the broken rocks half sunk in blue-green water, the lulling sound of whose splash and murmur reached us through the pine-branches. All at once the white monastery came into sight, and I was walking past the trickling spring, and the ravine full of plane-trees and fig-trees, and up the worn steps to the terrace with its one cypress, the sea, the sphinx-rock and the castle island beyond, and the *vounò* [mountain], with the mill glimmering palely in its cloud of olives and lemons and cypresses and walnut-trees. The courtyard of the monastery, with its thick round arches and cypress-shaded church and luminous walls, snowy and cream-coloured and blue in shadow, was heavy with the scent of orange-blossom. As I left, the first cuckoo, alarming and strange, called from the woods above. The light failed along the road back . . . You divined more than saw, the trees and rocks, and the poppies in the young grass. The streets were empty in Poros – the whole village was in church for the Entombment, and the streets and stucco houses and white staircases were quiet under thousands of low and bright stars, the lights sinking still reflections into the windless water. Later, from the window of the Averoff Hotel – where the toothless crone used to cackle us a welcome – I watched the hundreds of candles of the Epitaphios procession crawl along the sea-path from Galata, the reflections of fireworks flowering and fading and the drone of chanting, faintly crossing the water.

It is seven in the morning now, and all glitters and dances under a clear sky. Through the masts of the caïques, the Argive mountains unfold, the fleece of the olive trees grey-green and silver and gold where the sun touches them, the hollows and branching stream-beds a cloudy purple. Gulls float idly over the caïque sails.

Easter Sunday

Darling, I am again at the *narghiléh* café, quiet, happy, sun-drenched, and filled with the most terrible '*dor*' [longing] for you. Yesterday, I got Yanni to row me to the bay of Artemis, and lay in the sun all the afternoon, watching the shadows change on the island. Towards dusk, I shook myself, and walked through the wood where the white horse used to gallop aimlessly, and I used to talk of half-submerged vessels. Then through that sloping golden glade to the minute church, the narrow path till the place where the donkey used to pace round and round, drawing up the water, and up through the lemon-groves, to the mill. My darling, it was a moment I had been aching for, and, of course, dreading, for the last six years but, Boodle, there it was, as if nothing *had* changed; I stood and watched through the branches: Marina busy at the oven, Spiro, cheeks puffed with feigned and endearing exertion, emptying lemons into huge baskets – τά καλάθια – and a boy and a girl that I recognised as Kosta and Katrina, helping him. You can imagine the cries of welcome when I ventured onto the terrace, Marina smiling with her hands crossed on her apron, Spiro laughing and gesticulating with clownish glee. Evtychía is a thoughtful little girl of ten with dark bobbed hair and a mauve jersey. When kisses and greetings were over, all the talk was of you. 'When is she coming?' I said, Soon. We sat on the wall and talked for hours, (Kosta, still with those affectionate eyes and sweet smile, holding my hand proprietorially in his) of our old life: your pictures, my illness, the rat-bite, the night Hector got lost, climbing the walnut-tree, the Panegyri of St Panteleïmon, the autumn storm. The *magazi* [shop] is closed, as Spiro can get no wine, and as it got dark, I reluctantly said goodbye to them till the morrow, Easter Sunday, and wandered down through the trees to the Plaka where Mitso was waiting with his βάϱκα [boat], and over the still water to Poros. On the way down under the lemon leaves, I kept looking back for your long shadow, in blue trousers, white shirt and *bélisaires*, asking me to sing the Raggle Taggle Gypsies. Yanni our boatboy was waiting at the quay, and we went out fish-spearing with a carbide lamp on the front of the boat for a few hours, across that stretch of water between the Dragoumis and Tombazi houses. The bottom of the sea looked fascinating in the bright glare of the lamp – rocks feathered with anemones and prickly with urchins, octopuses and cuttle-fish coiled in the rock crevices, silver troops of fish lying silent two fathoms below, or darting off in alarm at the sudden lunges of Yanni's long, bamboo-shaped trident. He speared masses of them, and each catch was greeted with shrieks of delight by the two barefooted boys who were rowing. I got one *barbouni* [red mullet]. We got back in time to brush our hair, and join the swarm of Poriots [inhabitants of Poros] in the church for the Anástasis. There must have been 1,000 people in the square up the hill for the Resurrection, each eager face lit by its own candle. At the ΧΡΙΣΟΣ ΑΝΕΣΤΗ! ['Christ is risen!'] a great jangle of bells broke out, and the sputter and swish of fireworks, cannons firing at the fort, and all the candles danced up and down. *Adevărat a înviat!* ['Truly he is risen!'] Then to Yanni's house at the end of the village, a giant meal with clashing eggs, and back to bed, a bit drunk and very happy.

Today has been perfect too. I got to the hill early in the morning, having drunk two okes [carafes] of retsina with Yorgo and Stamatina, the shaggy little shepherd couple from the Vonnò, at the Plaka. We talked of our boiling day in that high desert, of all the water we drank as we lay panting under the plane-tree by the spring and the oleander bushes. They are as shaggy and small and brown and sly as ever, Yorgo with awkward hands resting on the shaft of his crook, Stamatina's pretty wrinkled face smiling out of its black headdress. She has a new papoose slung in a sort of leather sling from the saddle of her mule. They are as scorched and penetrated by the sun as a couple of cicadas.

At the mill, we had a huge banquet under the vine-trellis – paschal lamb and retsina and πατάτες φούρνου [baked potatoes] and onions and more retsina, and sang for hours. I made a fresh entry in our big white book (jealously hidden throughout the occupation, now the mill's pride and future heirloom), your health was most feelingly drunk by us all, Marina sang 'Kolokotrones' in her thin, true little voice, blushing like a girl at our applause. We danced terrific *Syrtos* and *Tsamikos* [traditional folk dances] (my hands still *ache* from the foot-slapping!), and all the time, the sun slanted down on us through the young vine-leaves overhead, and through its frame of vine and fig-leaves, our amphitheatre of orange and cypress and olive wavered down to the glittering sea and the island and monastery, and remembered bits of rock – lionlike and smoky as ever – on the blue looking glass that stretched away till it melted hazily with the sky.

I dived overboard and swam for a while in the cold sea on the way back and now sit at the old table, with the caïque masts thick in front, the salt flaking on my new-burnt arms, the sunlight still warm in my relaxed limbs and bones. This is where I wrote that first sonnet when you went to Athens, and I almost feel that tomorrow I will see you walking down the gangway of the Pteroté, in your grey wool Athens suit, silk shirt, blue-and-white tie, and small round white hat. The night is still and warm, friendly figures cross the golden light of the café windows like Karagosi men in their crisp *fustanellas*, and a mandoline and a zither sound their small tinkling cascade of music into the quiet air, answered by a lazy half audible *amané* [an improvised song in the Turkish style] from the steep white arched and staircased labyrinth of houses behind.

This is a kind and happy and simple corner of the world. All the misery and murder and *pumpute* [upheaval?] of the last seven years have shed themselves away like a hateful dream, and I am back for a few precious days in a glâbre [innocent], beautiful world inhabited by people like you and Pomme and Constantin and the two Alexanders and Guy and Prue. I send you, darling, all this. We must continue to hide here sometime, and feel that love and friendship are something separate after all, impregnably so, from the passage of time and its horrors and cruelties and callousnesses. I got your lovely letter, and am answering it when I get back to Athens tomorrow – many pages are already written. This is a parenthesis in it, designed to bring you the smell of the sea and of lemon-trees, and the love and greetings of all your friends in the island and Lemonodassos, and mine.

Hugs and kisses and *gouffis* to Pomme and Constantin and Ins [their daughter, Ina], and quite special *bessonnades* and hugs to Alexander M.; and to Alexander V.; and all, all that and more to you, my dearest darling, from

Paddy

It's intriguing that he mentions the other letter, already half-written. You wonder whether that did get sent – and whether he realised that this one, as well as being a 'parenthesis' to it, was also less authentic.

Maybe he wanted to get his impressions down on paper, as notes for a putative travel story, and Balasha was a convenient audience, already waiting to hear from him and familiar with the people and places he was talking about. That would chime with his tendency here to get diverted by the writing itself, lost in being a wordsmith.

Perhaps it was written out of duty – he wanted Balasha to feel loved still, but couldn't conjure up the passion of a decade ago. He's chivalrous enough to let her enjoy their shared memories, but you feel he's keeping it deliberately short on genuine intimacy, playing along with the idea of romance because he doesn't want to let her down. This way he can show fondness from a safe distance: by talking about 'love and friendship' in the same breath he is able to keep his options open, to shift the emphasis from one to the other rather than committing himself. Whereas the letters he was writing around the same time to Joan, his new love, are scattered with briefer, more immediate descriptions, and their real intimacy is evident.

But their friendship was lasting, and Leigh Fermor continued to correspond with Balasha until her death in 1976, sending her books, and offering help and advice when her life in Rumania got very difficult under the Communist regime – and his later letters, passing on family news and asking after her relatives, feel far more honest.

Deranged by love

Emily Dickinson's Master Letters

The 19th-century American poet, who wrote exuberant, metaphor-filled letters to friends and relations pretty much every day – many of them indistinguishable from poems – knew the value and significance of such correspondence. 'A Letter is a joy of Earth – it is denied the Gods,' she said in a poem of 1885. And, written as prose in a letter to one friend in 1868, and in verse form to another in 1882:

> A Letter always seemed to me
> like Immortality,
> for is it not the Mind alone,
> without corporeal friend?

Many of her poems were in effect unsent 'letters', actually written on envelopes (as well as on shopping lists, theatre programmes, paper bags, and other handy scraps) that would never be posted. And many of her letters later *became* poems – the point of crossover between the two is hard to find. 'What a Hazard a Letter is?', now published in *New Poems of Emily Dickinson*, was originally written in a letter to her mentor Thomas Wentworth Higginson in 1885, requesting news of her friend and fellow poet Helen Hunt Jackson, who was dangerously ill.

She never married, but – like another Emily of the same century – she wrote passionately about love. She apparently acquired a copy of *Wuthering Heights* in 1858, and developed several intense crushes of her own, her feelings not always being returned. In particular, her three mysterious Master Letters, written to an unknown man some time in the late 1850s and early 1860s (when Emily was about 30), and in which she refers to him as the Master and herself as Daisy, echo with the confusion and unhappiness of someone desperate to be loved and not sure how to do it.

But there is no evidence that she actually posted the letters at all: they only exist in rough drafts that leave phrases unfinished and alternative wordings not decided on.

Dear Master

I am ill, but grieving more that you are ill, I make my stronger hand work long eno' to tell you. I thought perhaps you were in Heaven, and when you spoke again, it seemed quite sweet, and wonderful, and surprised me so – I wish that you were well.

I would that all I love, should be weak no more.
The Violets are by my side – the Robin very near – and 'Spring' – they say, Who is she – going by the door –

Indeed it is God's house – and these are gates of Heaven, and to and fro, the angels go, with their sweet postillions – I wish that I were great, like Mr. Michael Angelo, and could paint for you. You ask me what my flowers said – then they were disobedient – I gave them messages.
They said what the lips in the West, say, when the sun goes down, and so says the Dawn.

> Listen again, Master. I did not tell you that today had been the Sabbath Day.
>
> Each Sabbath on the Sea, makes me count the Sabbaths, till we meet on shore – and (will the) whether the hills will look as blue as the sailors say. I cannot talk any more (stay any longer) tonight (now), for this pain denies me.
>
> How strong when weak to recollect, and easy, quite, to love. Will you tell me, please to tell me, soon as as you are well.

And then there is:

> Oh, did I offend it – [Did'nt it want me to tell it the truth] Daisy – Daisy – offend it – who bends her smaller life to his (it's) meeker (Lower) every day – who only asks – a task – [who] something to do for love of it – some little way she cannot guess to make that master glad –
>
> A love so big it scares her, rushing among her small heart – pushing aside the blood and leaving her faint (all) and white in the gust's arm –
>
> Daisy – who never flinched thro' that awful parting, but held her life so tight he should not see the wound – who would have sheltered him in her childish bosom (Heart) – only it was'nt big eno' for a Guest so large – *this* Daisy – grieve her Lord – and yet it (she) often blundered – perhaps she grieved (grazed) his taste – perhaps her odd – Backwoodsman [life] ways [troubled]

teased her finer nature (sense). Daisy [fea] knows all that – but must she go unpardoned – teach her majesty – Slow (Dull) at patrician things – Even the wren upon her nest learns (knows) more than Daisy dares –

Low at the knee that bore her once unto [royal] wordless rest [now] Daisy [stoops a] kneels a culprit – tell her her [offence] fault – Master – if it is [not so] small eno' to cancel with her life, [Daisy] she is satisfied – but punish [do not] dont banish her – shut her in prison, Sir – only pledge that you will forgive – sometime – before the grave, and Daisy will not mind – She will awake in [his] your likeness.

Wonder stings me more than the Bee – who did never sting me – but made gay music with his might wherever I [may] [should] did go – Wonder wastes my pound, you said I had no size to spare –

You send the water over the Dam in my brown eyes –

I've got a cough as big as a thimble – but I dont care for that – I've got a Tomahawk in my side but that dont hurt me much. [If you] Her master stabs her more –

Wont he come to her – or will he let her seek him, never minding [whatever] so long wandering [out] if to him at last.

Oh how the sailor strains, when his boat is filling – Oh how the dying tug, till the angel comes. Master – open your life wide, and take me in forever, I will never be tired – I will never be noisy when you want to be still. I will be [glad] [as the] your best little girl – nobody else will see me, but you – but that is enough – I shall not want any more – and all that Heaven only will disappoint me – will be because it's not so dear

The letters veer from one extremity of love to the other – from its ecstasy to its almost physical agony. She's buffeted by a love 'so big it scares her, rushing among her small heart – pushing aside the blood and leaving her faint'. Parts of the letters echo the searching, philosophical voice of her poetry. Other lines are unbearably coy and submissive, talking about herself in the third person ('Daisy . . . who bends her smaller life to his'). And quite a lot of it sounds downright deranged.

These three letters have inspired endless speculation about the intended recipient. It may have been the Reverend Charles Wadsworth, a happily married Philadelphia clergyman, whom she had heard preach and with whom she did correspond for some time (describing him as 'my dearest earthly friend'). Or Samuel Bowles, a journalist, publisher and friend of the Dickinson family, who – although contentedly married with ten children – was another a regular correspondent. Or even Otis Phillips Lord, a close friend of her father's and a judge on the supreme court of Massachusetts. He and Emily developed a close relationship after the death of his wife Elizabeth in 1877 (on Emily's 47th birthday), and some passages in their correspondence seem to suggest that they contemplated marrying, but he died in 1884, two years before Emily. (Wadsworth was 16 years her senior, and Lord 18, so they both fit the role of an older man or teacher, as 'Master' suggests.)

So why wouldn't she have sent them? Was it because she knew what a hazard they were – how they might be misread, what trouble they might cause? Or were they just exercises in composition, rather than written to a particular person? Whoever he was, and however strong her feelings, it still feels terrible that a woman of such ability and imagination should want to subjugate her own life so completely. 'Master – open your life wide, and take me in forever, I will never be tired – I will never be noisy when you want to be still. I will be [glad] [as the] your best little girl' doesn't square with her image as a feminist heroine, or with the ambivalence towards marriage that she expresses in poems such as 'She rose to His Requirements – dropt/The playthings of Her Life'. Is it possible that she felt this conflict for herself, and couldn't quite commit the letters to the post?

Love in three movements

Beethoven to his Immortal Beloved

Ludwig van Beethoven, composer of nine glorious symphonies, five perfect piano concertos and the most sublime chamber music (much of it after he'd lost his hearing), never married or had children, but did form various romantic attachments during his life. They were mostly with high-born women whose titles and social standing made marriage to him impossible, including the countess Giuletta Guicciardi, to whom he dedicated the Moonlight Sonata; the widowed Josephine von Brunswick, to whom he wrote a dozen or more passionate letters; and Therese Malfatti, possibly the dedicatee of the Für Elise bagatelle for piano, to whom he is believed to have proposed more than once. But for students of music and romance, the real interest is the woman who became known as his Immortal Beloved, whose identity, as the intended recipient of a famously unsent love letter, remains a mystery two centuries on.

She may have been one of the three afore-mentioned, but least half a dozen other names have been suggested over the years, among them Josephine's sister Therese von Brunswick, Dorothea von Ertmann (a gifted pupil of his), Countess Anna Marie Erdödy (a pianist who often performed his works) and the singer Amalie Sebald. The 1994 film *Immortal Beloved*, in which Gary Oldman's

Beethoven makes the mysterious lover his sole heir in his will, even proposed the theory that she was his sister-in-law Johanna, wife of his younger brother Carl. In fact the most likely candidate, according to researchers, seems to be Antonie Brentano, a Viennese aristocrat married to a Frankfurt businessman 15 years her senior, whose portrait was found with Beethoven's possessions after his death in 1827.

Whoever she was, he had some sort of romantic affair with her at the start of July 1812. Napoleon was marching into Russia, America had declared war on Britain for a second time, and Beethoven was in Prague, talking to Prince Kinsky about his annuity. (Ferdinand Johann Nepomuk Joseph Fürst Kinsky von Wchinitz und Tettau was a music-loving Austrian officer who, with two other aristocratic patrons, paid him an allowance.) He spent three days in Prague (during which Antonie Brentano and her family were also there, on their way to Karlsbad) before heading for the Bohemian spa resort of Teplitz, where he was going to take the waters and work on his eighth symphony (and, it transpired, have several meetings with Goethe, for whose play *Egmont* he had written the incidental music a couple of years earlier). And by the time he got to Teplitz on 5 July he was clearly in the throes of an all-consuming passion. The unsent letter, found among his papers on his death 15 years later, was written over the course of two days: a crescendo of devotion and a yearning for a love that seems to be already over.

6 July, morning

My angel, my all, my own self – only a few words today, and that too with pencil (with yours) – only till tomorrow is my lodging definitely fixed. What abominable waste of time in such things – why this deep grief, where necessity speaks?

Can our love persist otherwise than through sacrifices, than by not demanding everything? Canst thou change it, that thou are not entirely mine, I not entirely thine? Oh, God, look into beautiful Nature and compose your mind to the inevitable. Love demands everything and is quite right, so it is for me with you, for you with me – only you forget so easily, that I must live for you and for me – were we quite united, you would notice this painful feeling as little as I should . . .

. . . We shall probably soon meet, even today I cannot communicate my remarks to you, which during these days I made about my life – were our hearts close together, I should probably not make any such remarks. My bosom is full, to tell you much – there are moments when I find that speech is nothing at all. Brighten up – remain my true and only treasure, my all, as I to you. The rest the gods must send, what must be for us and shall.

Your faithful

Ludwig

Monday evening, 6 July

You suffer, you, my dearest creature. Just now I perceive that letters must be posted first thing early. Mondays – Thursdays – the only days, when the post goes from here to K [if this is Karlsbad, it reinforces the idea of Antonie as the beloved, especially as he joined her family there towards the end of the month]. You suffer – oh! Where I am, you are with me, with me and you, I shall arrange that I may live with you. What a life!

So! Without you – pursued by the kindness of the people here and there, whom I mean – to desire to earn just as little as they earn – humility of man towards men – it pains me – and when I regard myself in connection with the Universe, what I am, and what he is – whom one calls the greatest – and yet – there lies herein again the godlike of man. I weep when I think you will probably only receive on Saturday the first news from me – as you too love – yet I love you stronger – but never hide yourself from me. Good night – as I am taking the waters, I must go to bed. Oh God – so near! so far! Is it not a real building of heaven, our Love – but as firm, too, as the citadel of heaven.

Good morning, on 7 July

Even in bed my ideas yearn towards you, my Immortal Beloved, here and there joyfully, then again sadly, awaiting from Fate, whether it will listen to us. I can only live, either altogether with you or not at all. Yes, I have determined to wander about for so long far away, until I can fly into your arms and call myself quite at home with you, can send my soul enveloped by yours into the realm of spirits – yes, I regret, it must be. You will get over it all the more as you know my faithfulness to you; never another one can own my heart, never – never! O God, why must one go away from what one loves so, and yet my life in W. [Vienna] as it is now is a miserable life. Your love made me the happiest and unhappiest at the same time. At my actual age I should need some continuity, sameness of life – can that exist under our circumstances? Angel, I just hear that the post goes out every day – and must close therefore, so that you get the L. at once. Be calm – love me – today – yesterday.

What longing in tears for you – You – my Life – my All – farewell. Oh, go on loving me – never doubt the faithfullest heart

Of your beloved

L

Ever thine.
Ever mine.
Ever ours.

This, of course, is the letter that haunts Carrie Bradshaw in the first *Sex and the City* film, apparently highlighting the gulf between 'true love' and whatever Mr Big claims to feel for her. And it's those last three lines he whispers to her as they marry at the end of the film – although it would have scuppered the potential for a second film if she'd been satisfied with that . . .

Why wasn't it sent? It's clearly a farewell, and it has been suggested that Beethoven was contemplating killing himself (his hearing loss had started more than a decade earlier and in 1802 he had actually drafted a suicide letter – also unsent – to his brothers, unable to bear the frustration of not being able to hear his own music). Or perhaps he simply knows these are the last words he'll address to her as his beloved, because there is no possibility of a future together. She is evidently someone he could confide in ('my remarks . . . which during these days I made about my life'), but their affair definitely seems to be in the past ('Your love made me the happiest and unhappiest at the same time').

You can't help looking for musical references in the writing. Certainly the sense of experiencing extremes of happiness and unhappiness at the same time is something he is capable of evoking with music. There is a suggestion that distance makes communication impossible, that words aren't true enough, that his real feelings can only be conveyed through something more immediate: when he says 'I find that speech is nothing at all', is he thinking that music would convey more? It's even tempting to see the three sections of the letter as 'movements' of a musical composition.

And although the rhythm of the original German is lost in translation, those last three lines, with their repeated 'Ever', do feel like the calm, decisive resolution of some complex theme. Perhaps, if she was never going to be his in reality, this was the closest he could get to a kind of acceptance.

The torment of not knowing

Randolph Ash to Christabel LaMotte in A. S. Byatt's *Possession*

If love letters are evidence of the past, tracing their history is like detective work. The plot of Henry James's novella *The Aspern Papers* is constructed entirely around the narrator's obsession with tracking down a collection of letters from a Romantic poet. A similar fixation drives A. S. Byatt's Booker-winning novel *Possession*, where the search becomes a literary puzzle, unravelling the relationship between two writers. It's also a book about the oddness of opening *other people's* letters: trespassing on private territory and reading words never seen by the person they were meant for.

Roland Michell, researching the (fictional) Victorian poet Randolph Henry Ash in the London Library, comes across (and steals) two drafts, clearly incomplete and full of crossings-out, of a letter from Ash to an unknown but reclusive literary woman, later discovered to be a fellow poet, Christabel LaMotte. You can feel the urgency in Ash's voice in both these unfinished versions, his excitement at having met Christabel, and his uncertainty in how to address her.

Dear Madam,

Since our extraordinary conversation I have thought of nothing else. It has not often been given to me as a poet, it is perhaps not often given to human beings, to find such ready sympathy, such wit and judgment together. I write with a strong sense of the necessity of continuing our ~~intere~~ talk, and without premeditation, ~~under the impression that you were indeed as much struck as I was by our quite extraordinary~~ to ask if it would be possible for me to call on you, perhaps one day next week. I feel, I know with a certainty that cannot be the result of folly or misapprehension, that you and I must speak again. I know you go out in company very little, and was the more fortunate that dear Crabb managed to entice you to his breakfast table. To think that amongst the babble of undergraduate humour and through all Crabb's well-wrought anecdotes, even including the Bust, we were able to say so much, that was significant, simply to each other. ~~I cannot surely be alone in feeling~~

The second attempt is longer and more discursive: he's running ahead of himself and saying most of the things he would want to say if he saw her again, like we do when we chatter to a friend on the phone and realise we're using up the gossip we had planned to exchange on meeting.

Dear Madam,

Since our pleasant and unexpected conversation I have thought of little else. Is there any way in which it can be resumed, more privately and at more leisure? I know you go out in company very little, and was the more fortunate that dear Crabb managed to entice you to his breakfast table. How much I owe to his continuing good health, that he should feel able and eager, at eighty-two years of age, to entertain poets and undergraduates and mathematical professors and political thinkers so early in the day, and to tell anecdotes of the Bust with his habitual fervour without too much delaying the advent of buttered toast.

Did you not find it as strange as I did, that we should so immediately understand each other so well? For we did understand each other uncommonly well, did we not? Or is this perhaps a product of the over-excited brain of a middle-aged and somewhat disparaged poet, when he finds that his ignored, his arcane, his deviously perspicuous meanings, which he thought *not* meanings, since no one appeared able to understand them, had after all one clear-eyed and amused reader and judge? What you said of Alexander Selkirk's monologue, the good sense you made of the ramblings of *my* John Bunyan, your understanding of the passion of Iñez de Castro . . . gruesomely *resurrecta* . . . but that is enough of my egotistical mutter, and of those of my *personae*, who are not, as you so rightly remarked, my *masks*. I would not have you think that I do not recognise the superiority of your own fine ear and finer taste. I am convinced that you must undertake that grand Fairy Topic – you will make something highly strange and original of it. In connection with that, I wonder if you have thought of Vico's history of the primitive races – of his idea that the ancient gods and later heroes are personifications of the fates and aspirations of the people rising in figures from the common mind? Something here might be made of your Fairy's legendary rootedness in veritable castles and genuine agricultural reform – one of the queerest aspects of her story, to a modern mind. But I run on again; assuredly you have determined on your own best ways of presenting the topic, you who are so wise and learned in your retirement.

I cannot but feel, though it may be an illusion induced by the delectable drug of *understanding*, ~~that you must in some way share my eagerness that further conversation could be mutually profitable that we *must meet*. I *cannot*~~ do not think I ~~am~~ can be mistaken in my belief that our meeting was also ~~important~~ interesting to you, and that however much you may value your seclusion

I know that you came only to honour dear Crabb, at a small informal party, because he had been of assistance to your illustrious Father, and valued his work at a time when it meant a great deal to him. But you did *come out*, so I may hope that you can be induced to vary your quiet days with

I am sure you understand

There is an early sense of understanding here – the recognition of a fellow thinker, rather than an expression of any sort of passion – but Ash's evident disquiet in these incomplete drafts, his concern to say the right thing, reveals the depth of his feeling. The final draft, actually sent and later found (along with its reply) among Christabel's papers, is the shortest, but more assured and intimate, addressing her by name, mentioning it a second time and ending with an attractively tentative confidence.

Dear Miss LaMotte,

It was a great pleasure to talk to you at dear Crabb's breakfast party. Your perception and wisdom stood out through the babble of undergraduate wit, and even surpassed our host's account of the finding of Wieland's bust. May I hope that you too enjoyed our talk – and may I have the pleasure of calling on you? I know you live very quietly, but I would be very quiet – I only want to discuss Shakespeare and Wordsworth and Coleridge and Goethe and Schiller and Webster and Ford and Sir Thomas Browne *et hoc genus omne*, not forgetting, of course, Christabel LaMotte and the ambitious Fairy Project. Do answer this. You know, I think, how much a positive answer would give pleasure to

Yours very sincerely

Randolph Henry Ash

The whole book is an exploration of this mysterious relationship (which resulted in an illegitimate child) and a search – by Roland in collaboration with Christabel's great-great-great-niece Maud Bailey – for the poets' remaining correspondence. It ends with the discovery of a last letter from Christabel, written nearly three decades after she and Ash had parted acrimoniously, and with no certainty that he would ever read it: she sent it to Ash's wife, Ellen, when he was dying, leaving it to her to decide whether to give it to him.

Ellen had decided not to. But she had also found, sifting through the poems in his desk in the last days before his death, an unsent, unfinished, letter from Ash to Christabel. She knew about Christabel – he had confessed his affair to her 30 years earlier – but this is the written proof. And because the letter was never sent, it's Ellen who reads it: the wife, instead of the mistress.

My dear,

I write each year, round about All Souls, because I must, although I know – I was about to say, although I know that you will not answer, although I know no such thing with certainty; I *must* hope; you may remember, or forget, it is all one, enough to feel able to write to me, to enlighten me a little, to take away some of the black weight I labour under.

I ask your forgiveness freely for some things, of which I stand accused, both by your silence, your obdurate silence, and by my own conscience. I ask forgiveness for my rashness and precipitance in hurrying to Kernemet, on the suppositious chance that you might be there, and without ascertaining whether or not I had your permission to go there. I ask your forgiveness, above all, for the degree of duplicity with which, on my return, I insinuated myself into the confidence of Mrs Lees, and so disastrously surprised you. You have punished me since, as you must know, I am punished daily.

But have you sufficiently considered the state of mind which drove me to these actions? I feel I stand accused also, by your actions, of having loved you at all, as though my love was an act of brutal forcing, as though I were a heartless ravisher out of some trumpery Romance, from whom you had to flee, despoiled and ruined. Yet if you examine your memories truthfully – if you can be truthful – you must know that it was not *so* – think over what we did together and ask, where was the cruelty, where the coercion, where, Christabel, the lack of love and respect for you, alike as woman and as intellectual being? That we could not honourably continue as lovers after that summer was, I think, agreed by both – but was this a reason for a sudden pulling down of a dark blanket, nay, a curtain of sheet steel, between one day and the next? I loved you entirely *then*; I will not say now, I love you, for that would indeed be *romance*, and a matter at best of hope – we are both psychologists of no mean order – love goes out, you know, like a candle in one of Humphry Davy's jars, if not fed with air to breathe, if deliberately starved and stifled. Yet

Now if thou wouldst, when all have given him over,
From death to life, thou might'st him yet recover.

And perhaps I say that only for the pleasure of the aptness in quoting. That would have made you smile. Ah, Christabel, Christabel, I force out these careful sentences, asking for your consideration, and remember that we heard each other's thoughts, so quick, so quick, that there was no need of ending speeches –

There is something I *must* know, and you know what that is. I say 'I must know' and sound peremptory. But I am in your hands and must beg you to tell me. What became of my child? Did he live? How can I ask, not knowing? How can I ask, not knowing? I spoke at length to your cousin Sabine who told me what all at Kernemet knew – which was the fact only – no certainty of outcome –

You must know I went there, to Brittany, in love, and

care, and anxiety, for you, for your health – I went eager to care for you, to *make all well* as far as could be – Why did you turn away from me? Out of pride, out of fear, out of independence, out of sudden hatred, at the injustice of the different fates of men and women?

Yet a man who knows he has or had a child and does not know more deserves a little pity.

How can I say this? *Whatever became of that child,* I say in advance, *whatever it is,* I shall understand, if I may only know, the worst is already imagined and put behind me – so to speak –

You see, I cannot write it, so I cannot post you these letters, I end by writing others, less direct, more glancing, which you do not answer, my dear demon, my tormentor . . . I am prohibited.

How can I ever forget that terrible sentence cried out at the ghastly spirit-summoning.

'You have made a murderess of me,' was said, blaming me, and cannot be unsaid; I hear it daily.

'There is no child' came through that silly woman's mouth, in a great groan, in what mixture of cunning, involuntary exclamation, genuine telepathy, how can I tell? I tell you Christabel – you who will never read this letter, like so many others, for it has passed the limit of possible communication – I tell you, what with disgust, and terror, and responsibility, and the coiling vestiges of love gripping my heart, I was like to have made a murderer of myself in good earnest –

And there it breaks off, having become, by turns, a justification, a plea for forgiveness, a desperate appeal for information and finally a cry of despair. A love letter for – about – his unknown child, even if his love for Christabel herself has been corrupted by guilt and bitterness. The two lines of poetry quoted are from 'The Parting', the sonnet that aptly starts, 'Since there's no help, come let us kiss and part', by the 17th-century poet Michael Drayton – but, as he says, love that has died can have life breathed back into it. And he makes it clear that this is only one of many unsent letters he has written her.

So now Ellen knows about Christabel's child, too, although, like Ash, she has no idea what happened to it. Ash had asked Ellen on his deathbed to 'Burn what they should not see', and she fulfils his request by burning this letter – but spares the unopened one from Christabel, burying it in Ash's grave along with their own love letters. If she had opened it, she would have learnt that Ash had a daughter, Maia, who was brought up by Christabel's sister as her own, believing Christabel was her aunt.

At first it seems tragic to think that Ash never knew about his daughter. But in a postscript at the end of the book, backdated to 1868, we realise that Ash had come across Maia as a child, recognised her mother's likeness and given her a message to take back to her 'aunt' – which Maia forgot to deliver. And so the pattern of love *not said* is continued.

'You may never see this'

Phyllis Kelly to Private Eric Appleby

During the First World War, nearly 20,000 bags of mail crossed the English Channel every day, delivering letters, cards, and parcels to the men serving at the Front. Letters were frequently returned with 'Killed in action' pencilled on the envelopes.

Phyllis Kelly's last letter to her sweetheart, written from Dublin, towards the end of the Somme offensive, didn't get as far as that. Phyllis, the daughter of an Athlone solicitor, had met Eric, an engineering student from Liverpool who enlisted in the Royal Field Artillery in 1914, at a dance while he was training in Athlone, and they wrote to each other from March 1915 onwards. In September 1916, Eric took on the duty of writing to a comrade's fiancée to give her an account of his death. A month later, it was his own family's turn to receive bad news, in the form of a telegram saying that he had been dangerously wounded. Phyllis's response is racked with fear for him, and the frustration of not being with him.

28 October 1916

My own darling Englishman,

I wonder why I'm writing this, which you may never see – oh God, perhaps even now you have gone far away from your Lady – I wonder when another telegram will come; this knowing nothing is terrible, I don't know what to do. I simply have sat and shivered since your dad's wire came. It was forwarded from Athlone to Pembroke Road as that was the address we had given the post office. Mum brought it to Leeson Street. I was in my room unpacking and had just hung up 'Eric' over my bed, when the old maid came up to tell me Mum was downstairs and down I rushed. That anything was the matter never occurred to me until I saw her face. Oh my love, my love, what shall I do – but I must be brave and believe all will be well – dear one, surely God won't take you from me now. It will be the end of everything that matters because, oh Englishman, you are all the world and life to me. But I must be brave like you, dear, but the words of your dad's telegram will keep ringing in my head and squashing out hope. 'Dangerously wounded.' I say it over and over again till it doesn't seem to mean anything – when I came over to Pembroke Road with Mum, I tried very hard to pray but no words will come into my head, except 'Oh God, give him back to me.' This writing to you is the only thing that makes the waiting easier – everybody is very kind, I know, but I feel I would give anything to be by myself – I think I will go to Leeson Street now to see if there is another wire.

Before she could send her letter, a telegram came from Eric's father to say that he had died. Phyllis kept Eric's picture above her bed for the rest of her life: she never married.

II

Fate Intervenes

In the days after Black Wednesday, 16 September 1992, John Major wrote a letter to the Queen offering his resignation as Prime Minister. 'It wasn't one of those letters you write waiting for your colleagues to talk you out of it,' he admitted later, discussing the incident when the Black Wednesday papers were released in 2005 under the Freedom of Information Act. 'I was intending to resign.'

Britain had been forced to withdraw from its (brief, turbulent) membership of the European Exchange Mechanism that day, after failing to stop massive speculation against sterling – even with interest rates hiked to 12 and then 15 per cent. It was a huge humiliation for the UK in Europe, as well as shattering the Conservatives' reputation for economic management (a poll the following month showed their share of the intended vote had plunged from 43 to 29 per cent).

The decision to leave the ERM had been agreed at an emergency meeting with Chancellor Norman Lamont, Foreign Secretary Douglas Hurd, President of the Board of Trade Michael Heseltine and Home Secretary Kenneth Clarke, but John Major – who as Margaret Thatcher's Chancellor led the UK into the ERM in 1990 – accepted responsibility for the day's events: hence his resignation letter.

So why didn't he go through with it? His 2005 account suggests that fate took a hand in the form of cabinet colleagues: 'One or two very senior colleagues had some very trenchant arguments why it would be wrong,' he explained, with characteristic understatement. And he also remembers 'one or two people saying to me "Well, you took us in, we have come out, you had better stay there and put it right"'.

An interesting conclusion to draw, in the light of David Cameron's resignation after the 2016 EU Referendum.

Politicians, so vulnerable anyway to the turn of events, must be used to writing letters and memos that become inappropriate or redundant. Dick Cheney, vice-president to George W. Bush from 2001 to 2008, kept a signed resignation letter ready *in case* he became incapacitated. Diagnosed with a long-term heart problem, and knowing that, as he explained, 'there is no mechanism for getting rid of a vice-president who can't function,' Cheney took it upon himself to sign a secret resignation letter shortly after taking office. 'Basically', he said in an interview, 'I resigned the vice-presidency effective March 28, 2001.' The letter, stating 'In accordance with Section 20 of Title Three of the United States code, I, Richard B. Cheney, hereby resign the office of Vice President of the United States', sat locked in a safe, pending, for seven years and known only to a handful of people, including Bush himself. It was never needed, and at the time of writing (and following a heart transplant in 2012) he's still going strong, more than a decade after leaving office.

And Dwight D. Eisenhower experienced that blend of personal and state duty even before entering politics. As commander of all Allied forces in Europe during the Second World War, he had ultimate responsibility for the success of Operation Overlord, the invasion of Normandy by more than 300,000 servicemen that began on D-Day, 6 June 1944. The night before, at his quarters near Portsmouth, he wrote an address, ending 'We accept nothing less than full victory', to be broadcast to the troops before they embarked. But knowing how strong the defence would be, he was also prepared for the possibility of the landings failing, and drafted a second message, in pencil, on a sheet of 7 x 4½-inch writing paper which he folded away in his wallet.

> Our landings in the Cherbourg-Havre area have failed to gain a satisfactory foothold and I have withdrawn the troops. My decision to attack at this time and place was based upon the best information available. The troops, the air and the Navy did all that Bravery and devotion to duty could do. If any blame or fault attaches to the attempt it is mine alone.
>
> July 5

The pencil draft of the 'In Case of Failure' letter shows that Eisenhower was anxious enough to get the month wrong, and that the second sentence originally started 'This particular operation', but was changed to 'My decision to attack', to make his personal responsibility clear. More than 10,000 Allied troops, including nearly 5,000 Americans, were killed on 6 June, but by the end of the day Allied troops controlled 80 square miles of the French coast. The second letter was never needed.

President Nixon had a similar 'just in case' statement ready before the 1969 Apollo moon landings, to be issued in the event of the mission ending in disaster. It paid advance tribute to Neil Armstrong and Buzz Aldrin as heroic explorers who had sacrificed themselves in 'the search for truth and understanding', and declared that 'the men who went to the moon to explore in peace will stay on the moon to rest in peace.' He was able to file it away when the Apollo 11 crew returned safely. But 17 years later, in 1986, President Reagan did have to make a very similar speech, when the space shuttle *Challenger* was lost, and he talked so memorably of the crew having 'slipped the surly bonds of earth' to 'touch the face of God'. Perhaps those words, too, were prepared in advance, in case they were needed.

For those of us whose correspondence is more mundane, less dependent on world affairs, letters are more likely to be unsent because of some casual interruption. Just as the poet Coleridge was – or claimed to have been – interrupted mid-flow by the arrival of 'a person from Porlock' while writing 'Kubla Khan', we may lose our train of thought or find ourselves distracted when life gets in the way.

In 1942, Barbara Pym – later to become a Booker-shortlisted author – took nearly two months to complete a letter to her old university friend Henry Harvey (with whom she'd been half-requitedly in love at Oxford, and who became Archdeacon Henry Hoccleve in her first novel, *Some Tame Gazelle*) in Stockholm, where he was living with his wife and new baby. Barbara was based in Bristol, where for a while she did war service censoring civilian mail. She must have come across many letters that ended up unsent for reasons of national security, and her own letters had to be written in guarded terms to get past the censors.

She writes the first few paragraphs on 22 October. Then suddenly it is 'Tuesday 10 Nov', with the apology, 'Oh how ashamed I am, not to have finished this before now! I've been busy writing other letters.' She doesn't say to whom, but she does admit that her mind has been occupied with a love affair. She tells Henry about 'drinking in Bristol's nice pubs' and about going to see *Gone with the Wind*, and adds, 'Isn't the news wonderfully exciting' – which might be a censor-proof reference to the Allied victory at El Alamein a few days earlier. And she signs off with love to 'you and Elsie and "the baby"'.

But life evidently intrudes again, because it's not until 17 December that she realises it hasn't been sent, and apologises for probably being too late for Christmas now, 'what with censorship and everything – (happy Christmas to the Censors – I always think they must have a very arduous job especially at this time – bless them!)'.

Pre-email, maintaining contact with friends overseas demanded an exchange of letters that was particularly prone, diary-like, to interruptions and distractions. The author and editor Diana Athill, whose decades-long correspondence with the American poet Edward Field was published in 2011, when she was 93 and he 87, as *Instead of a Book*, wrote a letter to him on 23 November 2000, full of Booker Prize gossip, which she found still unposted a couple of weeks later, at the beginning of December.

(Diana Athill, incidentally, shares none of the neuroses that beset other letter-writers over the future of their correspondence. Noting that, legally, the letter as a physical object belongs to the person it was written to, but that its contents are the writer's copyright, in January 2003 she wrote to Field: 'My letters are yours to do what you like with. But not until after I die. I think, that way, I can avoid self-consciousness, since it will mean that the letters are now just another of the many things over which, once dead, I'll have no control, so there's no point in fussing about them.')

But writers of fiction, of course, can let fate play all kinds of games with the contents of their characters' letters. In *Alexander's Bridge*, by the 20th-century American novelist Willa Cather, structural engineer Bartley Alexander writes a long letter to his wife Winifred telling her he is going to leave her for his English mistress Hilda – but then drowns before posting it, when the bridge he is working on collapses. When, after his body is recovered, Winifred finds the letter in his coat pocket, its text is water-soaked and illegible, 'but because of its length, she knew it had been meant for her', and her belief in their marriage remains intact, unspoilt by his alternative plans.

It's a little like the film ending of *Brighton Rock*, where the teenage gangster Pinkie Brown makes that viciously cruel recording for Rose, the adoring waitress he has only married so that she can't give evidence against him: 'What you want me to say is "I love you". Here's the truth. I hate you, you little slut.' When Rose plays it, after Pinkie's death, the damaged disc gets stuck on 'I love you', repeating it over and over, and shielding her from the rest of his message.

Sometimes, fate takes a benign hand.

'This leaves me but one step to take . . .'

George III to the Prince of Wales about his abdication

Early in 2017, the Royal Archives released the draft text of an abdication speech that George III had planned to deliver in March 1783. It was the second time he had seriously considered giving up the throne and returning to Hanover, because of failures in the war with America and personal disagreements with members of his Parliament. This time, he found himself confronted by his worst nightmare – a coalition of his two least favourite politicians, Tory Lord North and Whig Charles James Fox. Given all this, George was sure enough of his intentions to write – alongside his speech – a letter to the Prince of Wales, explaining his reasons for resigning and in effect handing him the throne at the age of 21.

March 1783

The situation of the times are such that I must, if I attempt to carry on the business of the nation, give up every political principle on which I have acted, which I should think very unjustifiable, as I have always attempted

> to act agreable to my duty; and must form a Ministry from among men who know I cannot trust them and therefore who will not accept office without making me a kind of slave. This undoubtedly is a cruel dilemma, and leaves me but one step to take without the destruction of my principles and honour; the resigning my Crown, my dear son, to you, quitting this my native country for ever and returning to the dominions of my forefathers.
>
> Your difficulties will not be the same. You have never been in a situation to form any political system, therefore are open to addopt what the times may make necessary; and no set of men can ever have offended you or made it impossible for you to employ them.
>
> Your mother, whose excellent qualities appear stronger to me every hour, will certainly instantly prepare for joining me with the rest of my children. You may depend on my educating the boys in a manner that, if called into the British service, they shall not be undeserving of any marks of brotherly affection you may be inclined to shew them.

He didn't, of course, go ahead with this plan, and the letter was never sent. Despite the apparent optimism, in its wording, that the Prince of Wales would be able to make a decent fist of the job, in reality the King couldn't overcome his discomfort at the thought of his son George Augustus Frederick, the notorious gambler, womaniser and general profligate, on the United Kingdom throne (even if he himself had left the country and didn't have to watch . . .). One of the King's reservations about Charles James Fox was the bad influence his louche, spendthrift lifestyle (he could apparently swear in three languages) was having on the Prince.

You can't help wondering what might have happened if he'd subdued those misgivings, delivered the abdication speech – and sent the letter. What kind of King might the younger George have been if he'd got the job at 21 instead of having to wait another 37 years? Would he still have gone through with his 'secret' marriage to his Catholic mistress Maria Fitzherbert in 1785? Would he have had quite so much time to devote to partying and palaces and the commissioning of flamboyant projects such as Brighton's extravagant, multi-turreted Pavilion? Is it just possible that duty might have tempered his profligacy and irresponsibility – or would the additional power merely have given him more scope for excess?

As it was, he was free to continue fathering illegitimate children and running up massive debts as Prince of Wales, and then as Regent, until his father's death in 1820, when he finally became George IV at the age of 57.

Intercepted by an iceberg

Last letters from the *Titanic*

I've always found the story of the *Titanic* too upsetting to think about it. I can't watch any of the films or TV series, and have never even (or perhaps especially) seen the Kate-Leo-Celine Dion version. For me, it's just too sad to be turned into entertainment – it really happened, it's more than a special-effects opportunity. All those people setting off with so much hope, thinking they were embarking on bright new futures or holidays of a lifetime. And so many references that have lodged themselves in our consciousness: the icebergs, the deckchairs being re-arranged, the women and children first, the band playing on.

But having avoided all the films, I never knew that the ship was effectively a floating post office (RMS standing for Royal Mail Ship), with its own Mail Room deep on the lower decks and five staff who sorted the mail brought on board (over 3,000 bags) as well as dealing with letters posted by passengers and crew during the voyage. There's a memorial plaque to the five men in Southampton (originally in the main Post Office, until that closed; now in the Civic Centre, a minor tragedy in its own way). When, on the evening of 14 April 1912, they realised the Mail Room was flooding they attempted to move 200 sacks of registered mail to the upper decks, but failed.

The ship sank in just over two hours, with the loss of more than 1,500 lives and around 7 million items of mail. (Some *Titanic* obsessives have even calculated that those bags of unsent letters could have been used as flotation devices in place of missing lifeboats: apparently three bags would have been enough to buoy the average passenger, and all the bags strung together could have created a massive life raft.)

But a few letters, written on board and not yet 'posted' in the ship's postbox, survived the sinking – even if their authors didn't. One was found in the wallet of first-class passenger Alexander Oskar Holverson, after his body was recovered from the freezing waters of the Atlantic. Holverson, a prosperous Minnesota-born salesman, was returning to the US via the UK after a holiday with his wife, Mary Alice, in South America and Europe. Writing to his mother, he notes that 'This boat is giant in size and fitted up like a palacial hotel. The food and music is excellent.'

He mentions the American financier John Jacob Astor being one of his fellow-travellers (in fact, the richest passenger on board: he built the Astoria hotel in New York, and his cousin William Waldorf Astor, whose son had married Nancy Astor, built the Waldorf next door to it). 'He looks like any other human being even though he has millions of money. They sit out on deck with the rest of us,' says Holverson. And in a poignant note, he adds: 'So far we have had very good weather. If all goes well we will arrive in New York on Wednesday A.M.'

Mary Alice Holverson was luckier than her husband. She made it into a lifeboat and thence to safety, as did John Jacob Astor's wife Madeleine – and another letter-writer, Esther Hart, whose account of life on board is a little less blasé. Esther was travelling second-class, with her husband Benjamin and seven-year-old daughter Eva, from Ilford in Essex to Winnipeg, Canada, where they were going to run a chemist's ship. By an extra twist of fate, they had been booked on another ship, which failed to sail, and only transferred to the *Titanic* after Benjamin Hart kicked up an almighty fuss.

On board RMS '*Titanic*'

Sunday afternoon. [Esther didn't use the pre-printed '191-' to fill in the date . . .]

My dear ones all,

As you see it is Sunday afternoon and we are resting in the library after luncheon.

I was very bad all day yesterday. Could not eat or drink, and sick all the while, but today I have got over it, this morning Eva and I went to church and she was so pleased they sang Oh Lord Our Help In Ages Past, that is the hymn she sang so nicely, so she sang out loud, she is very bonny. She has had a nice Ball and a box of Toffee and a photo of this ship bought her today, everybody takes notice of her through the Teddy Bear. There is to be a concert on Board tomorrow night in aid of the Sailors Home and she is going to sing, so am I.

Well the sailors say we have had a wonderful passage up to now. There has been no tempest, but God knows what it must be when there is one, this mighty expanse of water, no land in sight and the ship rolling from side to side is very wonderful tho they say this ship does not roll on account of its size. Any how it rolls enough for me, I shall never forget it. It is nice weather but awfully windy and cold. They say we may get into New York Tuesday night but we are really due early on Wednesday morning, shall write as soon as we get there, this letter won't leave the ship but will remain and come back to England where she is due again on the 26th. Where you see the letter all of a screw is when she rolls and shakes my arm. I am sending you on a menu to show you how we live, I shall be looking forward to a line from somebody to cheer me up a bit. I am always shutting my eyes and I see everything as I left it, I hope you are all quite well. Let this be an all round letter as I can't write properly to all till I can set my foot on shore again.

We have met some nice people on Board and so it has been nice so far. But oh the long long days and nights – its the longest week I ever spent in my life.

I must close now with all our fondest love to all of you,

From your loving Est

Heaps of love and kisses to all from Eva xxxxxxxxxxxxxX

It's definitely a family letter – written in the kind of shorthand you can only use with people who know you well and will understand the allusions. The teddy bear referred to, which Eva was clutching when they boarded at Southampton, had been bought for her by her father at Gamages, the Holborn department store famous for its toy section. 'Oh God our Help' (as well as being terribly appropriate) was obviously a hymn with family resonance, and you get a sense of them feeling a little out of their depth socially: that 'I will send you a menu to show you how we live', as though menus (or at least the food listed on them) were not what they were used to.

And it's hard to think of Esther already feeling homesick, even before the ship gets into difficulty.

But it's interesting that, until the encounter with the iceberg, the letter was destined to come back with the ship and be posted on dry land in England. In the event, Benjamin woke his wife and daughter after the collision and got them into a lifeboat. He told Eva to hold 'mummy's hand and be a good girl', and gave Esther his sheepskin coat to wear. The two of them made it to New York, where Esther found her letter still in the pocket of his coat. Benjamin's body, if recovered, was never identified.

Esther and Eva returned to England to live in Chadwell Heath, east London (where there is now a Wetherspoon pub named after Eva). Esther Hart died in 1928 aged 65. Eva went on to become a magistrate and died in 1996 aged 91. In 2014 their letter was sold at auction for £119,000.

Forestalled by death

Havelock Ellis to Olive Schreiner

Who knows how many letters may have remained unsent – or unopened – because the writer or its recipient died too soon? Death is, after all, the ultimate intervention.

Writers Henry Havelock Ellis and Olive Schreiner corresponded by letter for nearly 40 years, having first met in 1884 when he wrote to her in admiration for *The Story of an African Farm*, her bestselling first novel, a coming-of-age tale of two cousins growing up in Olive's homeland of South Africa. She lived in Britain for much of the 1880s, during which time they established an intense intellectual (and possibly sexual) friendship, often exchanging letters on a daily basis. They were both unconventional, she in her liberal, feminist, political thinking; he writing groundbreaking books on sexual behaviour and attitudes, including *Sexual Inversion*, the earliest serious study of homosexuality, which was published in 1897, just two years after Oscar Wilde went to prison for it.

The friendship survived their respective marriages – hers, to cattle farmer Samuel 'Cron' Cronwright, lasted; his, to Edith Lees, prominent feminist and lesbian, didn't – and Olive's return to South Africa, where she became involved in politics, an outspoken critic of racism and imperialism. They met again when she moved back to Britain at the outbreak of the First World War, during which she was active in the peace movement, but ill health drove her back to Africa in August 1920.

This final letter, written to Olive in South Africa, is typical of their later correspondence, reflecting a shared instinct for landscape and the natural world rather than the intellectual intensity of their early years. Yet it also completes a neat circle, containing echoes of an early letter to him, and responding to the last postcard he received from her.

In 1886, while she was lodging at a convent in Kilburn, northwest London, she had written to him: 'It is so nice and quiet here. You can't think what a feeling of being far from the world one has. What happy peaceful faces most of these women have got!' Did he remember that appreciation of being 'far from the world' when he wrote to her, 36 years later, of Cornwall being even 'farther out of the world than you are'. Was there a recollection of her 'happy, peaceful nuns' in his image of elderly Spaniards retiring to meditate in 'some peaceful spot'? Her last postcard, written from South Africa in full awareness of her ill health, mentions that 'The heat here is very great, so oppressive – unlike that Alp-country heat.' In answer to which, his description of the 'wholesome & invigorating' Cornish weather, of being caught in wild gales with rain drops 'like small shot', seems to send cool, healing balm.

Wed 1 Dec/20

Dear Olive,

I am now in Cornwall for a few weeks or months & very pleasantly situated in a spot I have never been near before, on the north coast, about half way between Bude

& Newquay, not so very far from Tintagel. All along here is the finest rock (slate really) coast I have ever seen in Cornwall or perhaps anywhere, so rugged & fantastic with caves & islands & peninsulas, & there are of course no visitors about now, & very few natives live about here, so that I can wander about in the most magnificent scenery all day long & never see even a single person.

I expect it is farther out of the world than you are. I seldom see a newspaper & when I do I scarcely glance at it. The world doesn't matter when one is among real thing[s].

I have always understood so well how it was that Spaniards after a busy life in the world retired in old age to some peaceful spot high up among the rocks as at Monserrat not so very unlike this, to spend their last years in meditating & dreaming. I cannot conceive any greater luxury. And there is plenty of society, a great number of sea gulls, & herons & ravens & owls.

There's also a house, quite a large one, that faces the little bay, & here I dwell, with Bishop the painter (& a housekeeper who does all the work, & her husband who is away all day, a pleasant young couple). We meet in the morning for a solid breakfast, & then separate for the day, to meet again for dinner in the / evening (there is tea laid in the afternoon for whenever we care to go to it, separately). This I find [a] most admirable way of living, & in Cornwall it is also cheap, for my share of the expenses which ordinarily comes to well under £1 a week.

I have heard from Cron who asked me to advise him about staying in Spain. I advised him against Spain which he would find too difficult & uncomfortable, not knowing the language, & I suppose he has now started for Rome, which Bishop here, who knows it in winter, also recommended. – I am well content to be here & have not the slightest wish to go to [the] Antibes where Marguerite Tracy is & wants me // to come to her house. We get wild gales here sometimes & I was caught in one yesterday some miles away, & the rain drops felt like small shot, but it is wholesome & invigorating.

Havelock.

Whether his Cornish rain would have soothed her in the South African heat he never found out. His letter was sent, but was returned unopened, because it arrived after she had died.

Returned to sender

Franz Kafka's letter to his father

The nightmarish, torturous worlds conceived by the Czech-born Jewish author Franz Kafka (*Metamorphosis*, in which the luckless protagonist wakes one morning to discover that he has the body of an insect; *The Trial*, about a man being prosecuted for some unidentified crime) start to make sense when you read his *Letter to the Father*, an emotional 15,000-word address to successful Prague businessman Hermann Kafka, the man he blamed for his psychological struggles and personal neuroses. Written in 1919, five years before he died, it rails against Hermann's overbearing, intemperate parenting – and at his own inability to escape it.

It's the kind of thing countless teenage boys must have considered writing (including 19-year-old Charles Highway in Martin Amis's *The Rachel Papers*: see chapter III), but Kafka was no longer a boy. He was 36 and still tying himself in knots trying to understand what he saw as his 'failings', trying to reason things out, wanting to forgive – yet still unable to resist saying, 'but if you hadn't done this, I wouldn't have ended up like that'.

Even when he tries to say 'It's not you, it's me', it lapses into an 'It's not your fault – but' explanation: he keeps saying that he's trying *not* to blame his father, but can't stop himself, invariably returning to Hermann as the source of all ills, including Franz's failure to break free and marry. (He twice became engaged to the same girl without managing to go through with it, and only found a settled sort of love, setting up home with Polish-born teacher Dora Diamant, in the last year of his life.) This endlessly circular attempt to rationalise the matter demonstrates the underlying problem:

> Dearest Father
>
> You asked me recently why I maintain that I am afraid of you. As usual, I was unable to think of any answer to your question, partly for the very reason that I am afraid of you, and partly because an explanation of the grounds of this fear would mean going into far more details than I could even approximately keep in mind while talking. And if I now try to give you an answer in writing, it will still be very incomplete, because, even in writing, this fear and its consequences hamper me in relation to you and because the magnitude of the subject goes far beyond the scope of my memory and power of reasoning . . .
>
> As a father you have been too strong for me, particularly since my brothers died when they were small and my sisters only came along much later, so that I alone had to bear the brunt of it – and for that I was much too weak . . . From your armchair you ruled the world. Your opinion was correct, every other was mad, wild, *meshugge*, not normal. Your self-confidence indeed was so great that you had no need to be consistent at all and yet never ceased to be in the right. It did sometimes happen that you had no opinion whatsoever about a matter and as a result all opinions that were at all possible with respect to the matter were necessarily

> wrong, without exception. You were capable, for instance, of running down the Czechs, and then the Germans, and then the Jews, and what is more, not only selectively but in every respect, and finally nobody was left except yourself. For me you took on the enigmatic quality that all tyrants have whose rights are based on their person and not on reason. At least so it seemed to me.

So Franz grew up inhibited and insecure. And nowhere were his neuroses more of a challenge that in his attempts to get married – as he takes pains to explain:

> I showed no foresight at all concerning the significance and possibility of a marriage for me; this up to now greatest terror of my life has come upon me almost completely unexpectedly. The child had developed so slowly, these things were outwardly all too remote; now and then the necessity of thinking of them did arise; but that here a permanent, decisive and indeed the most grimly bitter ordeal loomed was impossible to recognise. In reality, however, the marriage plans turned out to be the most grandiose and hopeful attempts at escape, and, consequently, their failure was correspondingly grandiose.
>
> I am afraid that, because in this sphere everything I try is a failure, I shall also fail to make these attempts to marry incomprehensible to you. And yet the success of this whole letter depends on it, for in these attempts there was, on the one hand, concentrated everything I had at my disposal in the way of positive forces, and, on

the other hand, there also accumulated, and with downright fury, all the negative forces that I have described as being the result in part of your method of upbringing, that is to say, the weakness, the lack of self-confidence, the sense of guilt, and they positively drew a cordon between myself and marriage. The explanation will be hard for me also because I have spent so many days and nights thinking and burrowing through the whole thing over and over again that now even I myself am bewildered by the mere sight of it.

I venture to say that nothing has happened to you in your whole life that had such importance for you as the attempts at marriage have had for me. By this I do not mean that you have not experienced anything in itself as important; on the contrary, your life was much richer

(here we go again . . .)

and more care-laden and more concentrated than mine, but for that very reason nothing of this sort has happened to you. It is as if one person had to climb five low steps and another person only one step, but one that is, at least for him, as high as all the other five put together; the first person will not only manage the five, but hundreds and thousands more as well, he will have led a great and very strenuous life, but none of the steps he has climbed will have been of such importance to him as for the second person that one, first, high step, that step which it is impossible for him to climb even by exerting all his strength, that step which he cannot get up on and which he cannot naturally get past either.

You can see what Kafka means about bewildering himself with his own explanation. Ultimately, what it boils down to is:

> Marrying is barred to me because it is your very own domain. Sometimes I imagine the map of the world spread out and you stretched diagonally across it. And I feel as if I could consider living in only those regions that either are not covered by you or are not within your reach. And in keeping with the conception I have of your magnitude, these are not many and not very comforting regions – and marriage is not among them.

You start to feel mad yourself, just thinking it through.

In the final sentences of his letter, he says:

> Naturally things cannot in reality fit together the way the evidence does in my letter; life is more like a Chinese puzzle. But with the correction made by this rejoinder – a correction I neither can nor will elaborate in detail

(what, you wonder, does he think he's been doing for the last 14,900 words?)

> – in my opinion something has been achieved which so closely approximates the truth that it might reassure us both a little and make our living and our dying easier.

His mother evidently thought otherwise. According to Kafka's friend and official biographer Max Brod – the man he asked to destroy his writings after his death – Kafka gave the letter to her to pass to Hermann.

But Julie Kafka was in some ways a dubious choice as go-between. A devoted homemaker who wanted only to keep the family peace and didn't understand her son's creative ambitions, she is herself gently 'denounced' in the letter, for having, by her kindness, 'unconsciously played the part of a beater during a hunt. . . And then I was again the furtive creature, the cheat, the guilty one, who in his worthlessness could only pursue backstairs methods even to get the things he regarded as his right.'

Hermann would surely have deplored this new instance of his son's 'backstairs methods', despised him for not having the courage to hand over the letter himself. And how would he have reacted to its contents? If Hermann was so impossible to reason with, how could this have persuaded him of anything – let alone that he was in the wrong? Isn't the entire letter a testament to its own futility?

Anyway, Julie Kafka chose not to deliver it, and instead returned it to Franz. That decision, whether because she sensed it would be pointless and wanted to spare him the ultimate disappointment, or whether she felt that, far from reassuring either father or son, it might have made things even worse between them, now seems like divine intervention.

Overtaken by events

Iris Murdoch's *A Severed Head* and other novels

There's something wonderfully contrary in the way Iris Murdoch, Oxford classicist, philosophy tutor and Booker Prize winner, wrote page-turners that on a superficial level sometimes feel like unmissable TV drama – the forerunner of *Dallas* and *Dynasty*, as a friend of mine put it recently. Her characters have so many affairs and infidelities that they're forever having to write letters untangling arrangements, explaining themselves and analysing their own motives, and in the maelstrom quite a few of these end up unsent or mislaid. Especially as events and relationships proceed at such a dizzying pace that the whole picture can be reversed in an instant.

In *The Nice and the Good*, Jessica writes three frantic, pleading letters to John Ducane, the man she is obsessively in love with (and to whom she has recently been unfaithful). While debating which one to send, she receives an anonymous package enclosing a stolen letter to Ducane from another of his lovers, and a threatening reference to her own infidelity. Which rather distracts her from sending any of hers at all . . .

'Letters are dangerous,' says Hilary Burde in *A Word Child*, where letters are constantly being written, re-written, agonised over and hand-delivered all over London. And as if to emphasise their significance, Iris Murdoch's first novel, *Under The Net*, has an entire page devoted to the posting of letters at the General Post Office in King Edward Street (today the building is, sadly, part of Merrill Lynch Wealth Management), describing the 'great gaping mouths where one can watch the released letter falling down and down a long dark well . . . turning over and over like an autumn leaf', and where, after a long drunken lunch, her characters write letters purely for the pleasure of posting them. If you thought Anthony Trollope was preoccupied by all things postal, this is Trollope on acid.

In Murdoch's 1961 novel *A Severed Head*, the narrator, Martin Lynch-Gibbon, writes three versions of a letter to anthropologist Honor Klein (addressed variously 'Dear Dr Klein', 'Dear Honor Klein' and 'Dear Honor' as he debates with himself their level of intimacy) after a bizarre confrontation with her the previous night. He broods over these three – and is even tempted to write a fourth ('The notion of there being some further development of my thought which demanded expression became very compelling indeed') – before finally deciding, exhausted by his literary efforts, to mail the second version.

At the end of the novel, during the course of which every possible combination of couples is assembled and dismantled again ('The removal men seemed to have got quite used to moving the things to and fro'), Martin writes an emotional appeal to his long-time mistress Georgie. By this time, he's discovered that his wife Antonia has been having an affair with his brother Alexander, and that her former lover (and psycho-analyst), Palmer, is having an incestuous relationship with Honor (his sister), whom Martin has realised he himself is love with. Written at London Airport, where he's been waiting all day, to watch Honor leave for New York with Palmer, and written partly to distract himself from the knowledge that it will be the last time he sees Honor, it's appropriately wrung-out, desperate and verging on the hallucinatory: there's only so much drama any of them can take.

> My child, I feel as if we two are like survivors of a wreck, who have suffered so much together that they can hardly, thereafter, bear to see each other. It is indeed for some such reason that I have avoided you, and I have felt that on your side the same reluctance must exist to renew a relation which has occasioned so much torment. What has happened to us, my darling Georgie, since that day before Christmas when we lay together in front of your fire like two children in a wood? How much innocence we must have *had* then, as we have *lost* so much since! You may say that it is about time for the robins to come and cover us with leaves. Indeed I can hardly guess at your sufferings, considering how little I understand my own: nor can I guess at your bitterness against me, nor do I know whether anything remains between us which can be mended. I write this almost without hope of salvage, and yet I have to write; for I feel as if we had been actors in a play, and there must be some exchange between us for the drama to be complete. This seems a cold way to greet you, but I must be honest and confess to you how stunned and how half alive I at this moment feel. I must see you, do you understand, even if it is only to find out certain things uncertainty about which torments me; and yet with the hope, when we look on each other again in the solitude which this carnage has created, of more than that. Will you at least try, my Georgie, my old friend? If I don't hear anything from you to the contrary I will ring

> you up next week. We did really love each other, Georgie, Didn't we? In the name of that reality –
>
> M.

He puts the letter in his pocket and waits in the departure lounge, hiding behind a newspaper. 'I was not sure if the letter would do, I was not sure if it said what I felt, I was not sure what I did feel.' And he's about to become even less sure, because he then sees Georgie (who in another barely plausible twist has become a patient of Palmer's following a suicide attempt and a brief, broken engagement to Alexander) heading for the departure gate with him and Honor: brother and sister shepherding her between them. Martin's letter, whatever it was trying to say, is too late anyway.

Back in his flat, he finds the unsent letter still in his pocket, re-reads it and tears it up. It's hard to know what Georgie might have thought if she'd received it. Their relationship has been tough on her throughout, and Martin's feelings for her have lurched between the possessive and the non-committal: at one point he talks of wanting to 'put her in cold storage' and wonders 'whether my love for Georgie was strong enough to support the sheer weight and muddle under which I felt it now laboured'.

Would you want your ex-lover back on the basis that you're the only two people left at the end of an emotional bloodbath?

And besides, there's one last move to be made in this complex dance. Georgie and Palmer, it turns out, have gone to New York alone, and it's Honor who reappears at Martin's flat in the final pages. 'Could we be happy?' he asks her. And her reply, 'This has nothing to do with happiness, nothing whatever,' suggests that the blood-letting isn't over yet.

Casualty of war

A letter from the Front

Amid the awfulness of life in the First World War trenches, occasional moments of peace or beauty seem unbearably sad. It's the *Birdsong* effect: the novelist Sebastian Faulks's contention that the natural world remains 'utterly indifferent to the stupidity and cruelty of human beings', a rebuke to our mechanised horror. Yet it must have provided some solace to the soldiers themselves.

That's the sense you get from this letter, written by Second Lieutenant Henry Edward Otto Murray Dixon to his former commanding officer.

Murray Dixon, known to his family as 'Harry', was a wildlife artist – a pupil of Scottish animal painter and bird illustrator Archibald Thorburn – who joined up at the age of 30, was given a commission in the Seaforth Highlanders and went to the Front on January 5th 1917.

Typed on a wonky old typewriter complete with ink splodges and characters occasionally misaligned, the letter has an unfiltered simplicity, its writer interspersing the mud and the shelling with larks and kestrels and partridges taking off over No Man's Land. His family still has the pictures he mentions here.

Trenches.
6th April 1917

Dear Colonel MacFarlane,

I am sorry it is so long since you heard from me, as I know you want to hear how things go with me, but you also told me to do as much painting as possible in my spare time – and this I have been doing. I managed to get three black and white's done: 'Hooded crows on a french corn stack', which was in the *S.D.* [the *Illustrated Sporting and Dramatic News*, a weekly magazine] a short time back, (I hope you saw it) and since one of the Rats in the trenches and another 'Partings [baby partridges] in No Man's Land' – I was going across the open on a misty morning when they got up suddenly. Well I think both these will be in the *S.D.* as I've sent them to town.

I realise very fully indeed now, how very well off I was when at Ripon and under your command, these are precarious days! and will be yet more certainly so in the very near future, but I trust I may show a brave front when the time comes, its all very appalling. We have been out in No Man's land doing necessary work and the trenches approaching it are different to how they looked when we were last holding this part of the line! I think that the suspense and feeling of utter helplessness under heavy shell fire, is probably more difficult to bear up against and worse perhaps than will be the actual wound, or knock out blow, when it comes – perhaps if I had more of the true soldierly spirit I shouldn't feel it as badly, but its got to be gone through with now and shall be God helping me. There's a tremendous 'Straff' of the boches going on as I write – and such a sight, the bosche is landing a few heavies on my right a few thousand yds away, but is getting a terrible hammering.

. . .

The larks continue to sing right through heavy shelling and kestrels hover about, not at all concerned by all the noise it is very cheering to see them. There are some snowdrops and daffodils out in what remains of a garden close by where shells are falling constantly.

I came across a decapitated sparrow hawk yesterday and a Barn owl in another place, even the birds have to suffer, the rats flourish exceedingly tho'! The mud is very bad in most trenches now, but if the present sunny weather may only continue it ought to dry up. It is a curious business trying to dig standing in mud up to the knees and the spade clogged with wet mud which won't come off for throwing, and the trench sides falling in!

The Seaforths will do great things when the time comes and you will know I'll be trying to do my duty and proud to be of them!

I am, Sir,
Yours very sincerely,
O. Murray Dixon.

P.S. Do you see any prospect of a fairly early termination of hostilities? We can't help thinking it will be a long time yet.

Three days later, on 9th April, Murray Dixon was wounded at Vimy Ridge while mounting an attack alongside the Canadians. He died the next day, the letter still waiting to be posted.

III

Thought Better Of

Sometimes it's only after the letter is drafted, your thoughts put down on paper, that you realise it would be better not sent.

It may run the risk of fanning the flames rather than damping them down. It may, in the first flush of anger or hurt, have a resentful or overbearing tone that undermines your argument or obscures your purpose. It may change your own mind in the writing, persuading you of an argument you were trying to oppose. Or perhaps you know from experience that the recipient isn't going to respond well, or just won't take any notice . . .

And sometimes it's a question of self-preservation – an instinct that reminds you that you might regret it in future. Remember that you have no control over when the recipient will read it, what mood they'll be in, what other circumstances may colour the moment. Once it's sent it can't be retracted. There is a sense of committing yourself into the hands of Fate (who hasn't stood in front of a pillar box thinking, should I? Or shouldn't I?) that may halt you at the last minute. Characters in Anthony Trollope's novels – perhaps imbued with the author's own 34 years' experience working for the Post Office (as the man who imported the idea of the post box from France, he knows the significance of a letter) – are endlessly re-drafting them, worrying about their potential impact and frequently deciding not to send them after all.

There may be pragmatic, expedient reasons for filing the letter away, however great the provocation. In 1938, when a Berlin publishing house was negotiating to print a German-language edition of *The Hobbit*, J. R. R. Tolkien was suddenly asked to provide documentation of his Aryan heritage. Tolkien, naturally taken aback, replied to his own publisher, Stanley Unwin: 'Personally, I should be inclined to let a German translation go hang.' But as he didn't want to jeopardise the arrangement without Unwin's approval, he submitted two possible answers, to be forwarded as Unwin decided. One avoided answering the question altogether. The other made Tolkien's feelings very clear:

> If I am to understand that you are enquiring whether I am of *Jewish* origin, I can only reply that I regret that I appear to have *no* ancestors of that gifted people . . . I have been accustomed to regard my German name with pride, and continued to do so throughout the period of the late regrettable war, in which I served in the English army. I cannot, however, forbear to comment that if impertinent and irrelevant inquiries of this sort are to become the rule in matters of literature, then the time is not far distant when a German name will no longer be a source of pride.

It's not known which version Unwin sent but, as *The Hobbit* was eventually published in German, it was presumably the more anodyne one.

In 1962 Alfred Hitchcock, having agreed to do a series of interviews with fellow director Francois Truffaut, wrote Truffaut a letter demanding a chance to see the manuscript and change any passages he wanted before the publication of his book (with a default fee of $500,000 payable if Truffaut didn't comply with the agreement). Robert E. Kapsis's *Hitchcock: The Making of a Reputation* explains how publication was scheduled for a few months before the cinema release of *The Birds*, and Hitchcock's plan was for Truffaut's travel costs to be charged to *The Birds*' publicity account, which might have bought him some influence. But by insisting on paying his own costs Truffaut maintained his independence – and Hitchcock's letter remained unsent. Kapsis speculates that Hitchcock decided Truffaut's admiration could only enhance his reputation, and Peter Ackroyd, in *Alfred Hitchcock: A Brief Life*, points out that his request would have been 'a deep insult to a fellow professional'.

The thing is, letters freeze-frame a moment that won't last. As Carly Simon sings, in 'Letters Never Sent', one day they will feel incongruous and overdue: they have an odd, misfit quality that no longer makes sense. Even if they evoke how you once felt, by then it may well feel like another world, a lifetime ago.

And if our own letters will one day feel alien to us, we certainly don't want others to judge us by them. The American author and journalist Janet Malcolm, writing of the biographer's uneasy fascination with letters, cautions: 'When we are dead, we want to be remembered on our own terms, not on those of someone who has our most intimate, unconsidered, embarrassing letters in hand.'

Surely better, in many cases, not to send them?

'Now that I have seen the sentence, can I "unsee" it?'

Janet Malcolm to Jacqueline Rose

There are times, just occasionally, when we're tempted to keep an unsent letter rather than destroy it – and by keeping it, says Janet Malcolm, 'we are in some sense "sending" it after all.' *The Silent Woman*, her study of the relationship between Sylvia Plath and Ted Hughes, is also a book *about* biography. It goes beyond her subjects themselves, to explore the role and responsibilities of the biographer, the ethics of digging around in other people's lives – and the importance of letters as a way of tapping into the past: as 'the great fixative of experience', 'fossils of feeling'. She analyses other Plath biographies and talks to their writers, and in the course of this she writes a letter to the British academic Jacqueline Rose, whose own book, *The Haunting of Sylvia Plath*, was published in 1991. Having read it over, she then marks it 'letter not sent', and files it away.

March 18, 1991

Dear Jacqueline:

There was a moment during our talk in February that was like one of those moments during an analytic session when the air is suddenly charged with electricity, and what has ignited the spark is some small, casual, unconsidered action by one of the interlocutors. When you produced the passage from Ted Hughes's letter about literary criticism and the living and the dead, and I remarked on the sentence that I had not seen in Olwyn's copy of it, there was (and I will be interested to know if this description conforms with your experience) an almost palpable thickening of the emotional atmosphere. Your realisation that you had unwittingly shown me something you felt you should not have shown me affected us both strongly. As I thought about the moment later in Freudian terms, it seemed to me that issues of secrets and forbidden knowledge, as well as of sibling rivalry (the image of two women fighting over something – over a man?), had been stirred up. In addition, the moment raised for me the question of the place of morality in post-structuralist discourse. You value doubt and accept the anxiety of uncertainty – but you also have very definite notions of what is right and wrong. You immediately felt it wrong to 'give' me what Ted Hughes had 'given' you. When you asked me not to quote the sentence I should not have seen, you used the word 'ethically'. Doesn't the very idea of ethics imply a standard, a norm, a canon of acceptable behaviour? And

> isn't there some discontinuity between your position as a post-structuralist literary theorist and your attentiveness to the requirements of living in the world as a morally scrupulous person? Finally (and more directly to the point of our respective Plathian enterprises), doesn't this tiny incident of suppression in a sense reproduce the larger suppressions of the Hugheses? Now that I have seen the sentence, can I 'unsee' it?

'Can I unsee it?' That's the heart of the whole thing. She can't unsee the sentence in Ted Hughes's letter – it's already out there. As is her own letter to Jacqueline: it may be unsent, but the fact that she wrote it – and kept it – gives it a life, a presence, of its own.

She has already addressed the envelope when she decides not to send it. And although the questions it poses could be rhetorical, her comment, 'I will be interested to know if this description conforms with your experience,' is definitely future tense rather than conditional: she is clearly, at this stage, anticipating a response. It's almost as though what starts as a direct appeal to the intended recipient turns into a debate with herself: questions that she initially addresses to Jacqueline Rose become subjects for her own consideration, and she no longer needs to put them to Jacqueline.

'Neither the writing nor the not sending is remarkable,' says Janet Malcolm, 'but the gesture of keeping the message we have no intention of sending is . . . We are not relinquishing our idea or dismissing it as foolish or unworthy (as we do when we tear up a letter); on the contrary, we are giving it an extra vote of confidence. We are, in effect, saying that our idea is too precious to be entrusted to the gaze of the actual addressee, who may not grasp its worth, so we "send" it to his equivalent in fantasy, on whom we can absolutely count for an understanding and appreciative reading.'

Yet, writing two years later about that letter and the meeting that prompted it, Janet Malcolm no longer has any 'objective trace' of the interaction between her and Jacqueline, and admits she can't be sure that her letter is an accurate guide to what happened. It may be a fossil of feeling, but not necessarily of fact.

Five eye operations, two pneumonias and a ruptured appendix

James Thurber to Ernest Hemingway

The writer and cartoonist James Thurber became friends with Ernest Hemingway in the 1930s. Both hard-drinking and quotable, they maintained a warm relationship for decades (the last line of this letter includes an affectionate reference to Hemingway's *The Sun Also Rises*). Thurber's biographer Burton Bernstein describes him as being 'fond of writing cheer-up letters'. But it's hard to imagine what he thought might cheer his friend up in this one, except the line about 'sugar in your urine and a murmur in your heart', which is brilliant. Perhaps he thought that recounting his own numerous ailments, and his recovery from them, would distract Hemingway from his own depression and illnesses, and there is a dark humour in his dry, unvarnished accounts of conversations with doctors, even when referring to the loss of his own sight, which began with a childhood accident. Anyway, he was dissuaded from sending it by his wife, Helen, who probably knew what she was doing.

[11 January 1961]

Dear Ernest:

This is what the gals call a chatty letter intended to cheer, and not to be answered until you and I meet at Tim Costello's, – one, ten or twenty years from now, and the sooner the better . . .

This has been the damnedest November and December for friends of mine, and for me, too, in my memory. Everyone of us, though, began to pick up again during the first week of January. I have been doing some research about the cycle of ailments and moods in the human being, and have found out that the medical men, as well as psychiatrists, have become aware of seasonal phases of the body and the mind. It is now known that stomach ulcers increase greatly in November and, as for the mind, 'the winter of our discontent', just scratches the melancholy surface. I believe that all of us, especially the men, are manic-depressives, but only a small percentage are malignant ones. My friend, Elliott Nugent, was hard hit by his cycle this November, but he is putting up a good fight. He used to get hit worse in March, which rates second among the bad months.

A few years ago I wrote Ross's Boston doctor [Harold Ross was editor of the *New Yorker* magazine, for which Thurber wrote for many years], Sarah Jordan, about the cyclical nature of Man and said that I believed that it also affected ability and skill, but that each person had his own timetable. I suggested that there are periods when surgeons should not be allowed to operate. She wrote back that the psychiatrists agreed with me, but the surgeons did not. I never write like an angel, but I have recurrent phases when I write like a charwoman . . .

In 1931 I had a medical examination for insurance at the *New Yorker*. A few days later I met my insurance agent on the street. He had approached me shaking his head and said, 'You have sugar in your urine and a murmur in your heart.' 'That's not a diagnosis,' I said, 'that's a song cue.'

A few months later another examination showed no sugar and no murmur. My great eye doctor, Gordon M. Bruce, who lost half his hearing but won two silver stars in the South Pacific, told me, 'Only the reputation of the greatest doctor could survive you.' What he meant was after my left eye was shot out with an arrow, when I was seven, the sight of the other eye was completely destroyed about a year later. 'You lost the apparatus of vision,' he said, 'but you just went on seeing anyway.' 'You can call it God or ESP.' Then he said, 'I can't believe God wanted you to do those drawings.' I reminded him that God had drawn the kangaroo, the human being, to mention only two, which proved that God has a comic sense.

This kind of thing seems to happen more and more often and the baffled doctors are not very crazy about it. When I was nineteen, a Columbus eye doctor told me, very irritably, 'I suppose you could play the piano with both hands cut off at the wrists.' I talk quite a lot nowadays to doctors I know who are continually puzzled by cases of regression of disease. Two years ago the *Herald-Tribune* reported fifty-four cases of total regression of incurable cancer. All they need to do now is to find out the secret, and there are many good men working on it.

I still have personal physicians who stick to me when I am down, which I rarely am any more. I guess I got it all over with between forty-five and fifty-seven and, boy, was the scroll charged with punishments. I had five eye operations in eight months, two pneumonias, ruptured appendix with peritonitis, a plus 60 hyper-thyroid, an allergy that made me sneeze about three hours at a stretch and a nervous crack-up during which I pulled out of a castration complex with the psychiatrists. This amazed the psychiatrists I have talked to, none of them professionally, though. One doctor said with a sigh, 'We just mark the chart atypical.' He had called on me in 1942 when I was running a temperature of 103 and a pulse rate of 122. You name the pulse rate, Ernest, and I have had it. This doctor told my wife, privately, he was sure I had endocarditis. 'Nonsense,' said Helen. 'His temperature and pulse will be normal tomorrow.' They were, too.

If all this wasn't so damned reassuring, I wouldn't go into it, but God knows you have pulled out of things, too, and always will. Let's have some drinks together on New Year's Eve, 1980. Your luck, she is always with you, and I know you are not jealous that I share her with you.

One final anecdote about the docs. My appendix ruptured at six a.m. in November, 1944, and I wasn't operated on until nine o'clock that night. We were at The Homestead in Hot Springs, Virginia. The assistant surgeon who came to the hotel called my doctor in New York. He told him, 'This patient has not been nauseated, but he is hungry!' I don't know what my doctor said, but I can guess. I was taken to a hospital thirty miles away, in the only ambulance available, a hearse. When after three weeks, I got out of bed and dressed and went home, old Dr Emmett said, 'We thought you were gone. How do you account your putting on your clothes and leaving here?' 'I always dress before I go out into the street,' I told him. 'I am romantic.'

The other night I dreamed that you and I were walking toward a sunset and suddenly the sun began to rise. Reminds me of a favourite book of mine. But, then, I had the same dream about two other men, when they were down, Carl Sandburg and Robert Frost. Carl was eighty-three on January 6 and Frost is even older. God bless you and keep you. I'll see you in 1980.

As always,

James Thurber (44)

His valediction was optimistic, as neither of them made it to 1980. Hemingway killed himself five months after this letter *wasn't* sent – and Thurber died from a stroke at the end of the same year.

What need was there for any letter?

Anthony Trollope's *The Eustace Diamonds*

It would be satisfying to find a template for the *type* of person who dithers over posting a letter. But two of Anthony Trollope's most significant non-senders, Lucy Morris and Lizzie Eustace in *The Eustace Diamonds*, the third of his Palliser novels, couldn't be further apart in character. Lizzie, Lady Eustace, is scheming and selfish: she's already acquired a title from her first husband and, now widowed, is looking for money and security in a replacement. Lucy, sweet and steadfast, is half-engaged to Lizzie's cousin, barrister-turned-MP Frank Greystock (he has told her he loves her, but hasn't quite asked her to marry him, and might not be able to because she is a penniless governess).

When Frank does get round to proposing to Lucy, he does it in writing, and then sits looking at his letter, realising that, 'If he should decide on posting it, then would that life in Belgravia-cum-Pimlico, – of which in truth he was very fond, – be almost closed for him.' Finally (and Trollope is, naturally, brilliant at the ins and outs of the postal service), Frank drops it 'into a pillar letter-box just outside the gate. As the envelope slipped through his fingers, he felt that he had now bound himself to his fate.'

Lucy accepts him without hesitation, but the story can't be as straightforward as that, and before they get their happy ending she does the classic penniless-governess thing of offering to remove herself as an obstacle to Frank's career. Aware of her unsuitability – and of rumours that Frank has been unfaithful to her with Lizzie Eustace – she writes to him:

> My dear Frank,
>
> It is a long time since we met; – is it not? I do not write this as a reproach; but because my friends tell me that I should not continue to think myself engaged to you. They say that, situated as you are, you cannot afford to marry a penniless girl, and that I ought not to wish you to sacrifice yourself. I do understand enough of your affairs to know that an imprudent marriage may ruin you, and I certainly do not wish to be the cause of injury to you. All I ask is that you should tell me the truth. It is not that I am impatient; but that I must decide what to do with myself when I leave Lady Linlithgow.
>
> Your most affectionate friend,
>
> Lucy Morris.
> March 2, 18 – .

She reads this letter over and over again during the subsequent chapters, but never quite gets round to sending it, realising that, if he does mean to throw her over, she won't honestly care what happens to her. 'All to her would be ruin. And then, why should she lie to him as she would lie in sending such a letter?' Even when she hears 'from all sides' that he has deserted her, she doesn't send it. 'To communicate her thoughts to him was worse than agony. It would be almost madness. What need was there for any letter?

If the thing was done, it was done . . . At last she resolved that there should be no letter.' She destroys her note, wisely keeps quiet and waits for him to realise, as he eventually does, that she's the one for him.

Lizzie, meanwhile has managed to get herself engaged to another politician, dull but honourable Lord Fawn. But Fawn is already worried that Lizzie might be more trouble than he needs and writes to her, after much procrastination – 'on a Wednesday, which with him had something of the comfort of a half-holiday, as on that day he was not required to attend Parliament' – to tell her that he's no longer sure their marriage is a good idea. Although he's blunt enough to tell her that 'I could not go to the altar with you without fear and trembling', he's too honourable to actually break the engagement himself. 'As, however, I do consider that I am bound to keep my engagement to you if you demand that I shall do so, I leave the matter in your hands for decision.'

Weighing up the letter's potential before posting it, Fawn satisfies himself that 'it was impossible that any woman after reading it should express a wish to become the wife of the man who wrote it'. But Lizzie is in a tight spot and can't afford to let him walk away. Her two unsent replies both come into the Thought-Better-Of category, in the sense that she hesitates because she's sure she can think of a *better* response. The first – 'My dear Lord Fawn. As we have been engaged to marry each other, and as all our friends have been told, I think that the thing had better go on' – is all she can manage to start with, in her determination to hang onto the idea of becoming Lady Fawn. But two days later she still hasn't sent it. 'What was she to get by marrying a man she absolutely disliked?' she muses. 'Even stability may be purchased at too high a price.' Her second draft is therefore in a different vein and takes a little longer to write.

My Lord, –

I do not know how to acknowledge with sufficient humility the condescension and great kindness of your lordship's letter. But perhaps its manly generosity is more conspicuous than either. The truth is, my lord, you want to escape from your engagement, but are too much afraid of the consequences to dare to do so by any act of your own; – therefore you throw it upon me. You are quite successful. I don't think you ever read poetry, but perhaps you may understand the two following lines: –

'I am constrained to say, your lordship's scullion
Should sooner be my husband than yourself.'

I see through you, and despise you thoroughly.

E. Eustace.

Lizzie is in the process of comparing the two answers, pleased with the scullion quotation (from the 19th-century dramatist Sir Henry Taylor) but 'very much in doubt as to which should be sent', when a visit from a policeman brings the diamond necklace of the book's title (a family heirloom to which she has no claim, but which she refuses to relinquish) forcibly into the foreground of the plot, promising unwelcome publicity that will almost certainly make Lord Fawn withdraw his offer unless she accepts it swiftly.

Which version should she send? 'Or should she write a third explaining the whole matter in sweetly piteous feminine terms, and swearing that the only remaining feeling in her bosom was a devoted affection to the man who had now twice promised to be her husband?'

She plans this third draft overnight, but, 'Alas! she took one night too many.' The morning brings a new letter from Fawn 'receding' from his proposition altogether. At which point Lizzie finally gets a satisfying rejection ('No earthly consideration would induce me to be your wife') written – and sent – but pre-dates it to appear as though it had been composed several days earlier, in response to his original letter.

It's a complex game of timing and second-guessing, and Lizzie gets her timing wrong. In the final chapters, battered by public disapproval and the stress of a court summons over the diamonds, she engages herself to marry a man described as a cad and an imposter and probably a bigamist, but who plays in the same league as her. She sees his grasping ambition as a useful social tool; he knows he's catching her at her most vulnerable. And their agreement is arrived at without the involvement of letters, sent or unsent.

'Now I'm going to hit the bastard with everything'

Charles Highway to his father in Martin Amis's *The Rachel Papers*

Martin Amis seems to have been lucky in his parents. Two mothers, one who gave him a happy early childhood and also looked after his father in old age, even though she was by that time married to someone else; and a stepmother, Elizabeth Jane Howard, who turned him on to books (and got him into Oxford) by giving him *Pride and Prejudice* to read as a teenager. But he did have to go through his father leaving one of them for the other, so although he adored and respected Kingsley Amis – read his memoir *Experience* for the raw grief he felt on his death, and their shared delight in playing with language – there's presumably quite a bit of Kingsley in Gordon Highway, philandering father of the central character in Martin's first novel, published when he was 24.

The Rachel Papers is constructed hour by hour through the course of various days, but bookended by the fact that Charles Highway will be 20 tomorrow – 20 being 'the end of youth'. Angry, resentful, jealous of his sexually successful father, consumed by teenage angst, and fired up by reading D. H. Lawrence, Philip

Larkin and Franz Kafka ('to find a world full of the bizarre surfaces and sneaky tensions with which I was always trying to invest my own life'), he starts a letter to his father to which he adds throughout the book.

> I *think* it was that afternoon I began work on the Letter to My Father, a project which was to take up many a spare moment over the following weeks.
>
> Now, I thought, assembling fountain-pen, inkpot and notes, I'm really going to hit the bastard with everything. Forty minutes later I had written:
>
> Dear Father,
> This has not been an easy letter to write.

Every now and then Charles works on it a bit more, at one point changing the heading from Letter to Speech. After a particularly awkward encounter with Gordon and his mistress, and anticipating a weekend with Rachel at his parents', he fantasises, while attending a maths class at his Oxbridge crammer, about having some kind of showdown with his father: 'During the lesson, under the pretence of making notes, I planned the weekend – anecdotes about the village, nature speeches – and outlined a brief coda to the (by now) 2,000-word Speech to My Father.'

By the end of the book, he's got his place at Oxford and slept with Rachel, and dumped her. By letter – how else? Three hours' work to achieve the right level of spontaneity:

> My dearest Rachel,
>
> I don't know how anyone has ever managed to write this kind of letter – anyone who does is a coward and a shit and used it dishonestly, so I can only minimise all three of these by being as candid as possible. I got a feeling some weeks ago that what I felt for you was changing. I wasn't sure what the feeling was, but it wouldn't go away and it wouldn't change into anything else. I don't know how or why it happens; I know that it's the saddest thing in the world when it does.
>
> But it is I who have changed, not you. So let me hope you feel (as I do) that it has been worth it, or that it will turn out to have been worth it, and let me beg your forgiveness. You are the most important thing that has ever happened to me. C.

Reading it through, he notes:

> There was a pleasingly unrehearsed air about the repetition of 'feeling' and 'feel' and of 'changing' and 'changed'. That 'it is I' seemed rather prissy; perhaps 'it's me' would have been a bit beefier and . . . more modest. And I still can't decide whether all the 'it's' and 'don'ts' are nastily groovy or nicely Robert Frost. But, so far as I know, Rachel is not a fastidious reader.

And having put the letter in an envelope he actually speaks to her on the phone and tells her he loves her before going out to post it. But he *does* post it.

After which he has to deal with the other letter.

> The Letter to My Father – what a remarkable document it is. Lucid yet subtle, persistent without being querulous, sensible but not unimaginative, elegant? yes, florid? no. Ah, if Knowd-all could have read this. [It was Dr Knowd who had interviewed him for his place to read English at Oxford, and whom Charles dismisses as inconsequential because he misuses 'hopefully'.] The only question is: what do I do with it?'

In the last few pages of the book, Charles finds a sort of accommodation with his father, as they discuss his university entrance, and his break-up with Rachel, and even his parents' relationship, in an attempt at man-to-man bluffness, with Charles realising that the effort it takes to be constantly subversive, to sneer at older people and their ability to compromise, is exhausting and pointless, 'and that you're no better'.

He's actually got the letter with him, having taken it on the off-chance that it might be an opportunity to hand it over, but in the end, just before midnight marks his 20th birthday, and after a final meeting with Rachel during which she cries a lot, he drops the letter in the bin on top of her tear-stained tissues.

> Three minutes to go. I return to the wastepaper basket and find Rachel's mascara-ed ball beneath the layers of tissue steeped in my own snot and tears. I examine it, then let it fall noiselessly from my hand. I cover it now with the Letter to My Father.

So we never get to know what it actually said, but, given that he'd been reading Kafka, we can probably guess. Studying Kafka at school, the 18-year-old Amis described him in a letter to his father and step-mother as a 'fucking fool', so perhaps he allowed Charles to develop the same opinion. (See chapter II for Kafka's own unsent *Letter to the Father*, written in 1919.)

On Middlebrow

Virginia Woolf to the *New Statesman*

In October 1932, a newspaper review by J. B. Priestley of Virginia Woolf's second *Common Reader* collection of essays repeated Arnold Bennett's description of her as 'the High Priestess of Bloomsbury', and referred to 'terrifically sensitive, cultured, invalidish ladies with private means'. This sparked a series of radio broadcasts and magazine features debating highbrow versus lowbrow, which eventually goaded Virginia Woolf herself to write this letter to the *New Statesman*:

To THE EDITOR OF THE "NEW STATESMAN",
October 1932

Sir,

Will you allow me to draw your attention to the fact that in a review of a book by me (October) your reviewer omitted to use the word Highbrow? The review, save for that omission, gave me so much pleasure that I am driven to ask you, at the risk of appearing unduly egotistical, whether your reviewer, a man of obvious intelligence, intended to deny my claim to that title? I say 'claim', for surely I may claim that title when a great critic, who is also a great novelist, a rare and enviable combination, always calls me a highbrow when he condescends to notice my work in a great newspaper; and, further, always finds space to inform not only myself, who know it already, but the whole British Empire, who hang on his words, that I live in Bloomsbury? Is your critic unaware of that fact too? Or does he, for all his intelligence, maintain that it is unnecessary in reviewing a book to add the postal address of the writer?

His answer to these questions, though of real value to me, is of no possible interest to the public at large. Of that I am well aware. But since larger issues are involved, since the Battle of the Brows troubles, I am told, the evening air, since the finest minds of our age have lately been engaged in debating, not without that passion which befits a noble cause, what a highbrow is and what a lowbrow, which is better and which is worse, may I take this opportunity to express my opinion and at the same time draw attention to certain aspects of the question which seem to me to have been unfortunately overlooked?

Now there can be no two opinions as to what a highbrow is. He is the man or woman of thoroughbred intelligence who rides his mind at a gallop across country in pursuit of an idea. That is why I have always been so proud to be called highbrow. That is why, if I could be more of a highbrow I would. I honour and respect highbrows. Some of my relations have been highbrows; and some, but by no means all, of my friends. To be a highbrow, a complete and representative highbrow, a highbrow like Shakespeare, Dickens, Byron, Shelley, Keats, Charlotte Brontë, Scott, Jane Austen, Flaubert, Hardy or Henry James – to name a few highbrows from the same profession chosen at random – is of course beyond the wildest dreams of my imagination. And, though I would cheerfully lay myself down in the dust and kiss the print of their feet, no person of sense will deny that this passionate preoccupation of theirs – riding across country in pursuit of ideas – often leads to disaster. Undoubtedly, they come fearful croppers. Take Shelley – what a mess he made of his life! And Byron, getting into bed with first one woman and then with another and dying in the mud at Missolonghi. Look at Keats, loving poetry and Fanny Brawne so intemperately that he pined and died of consumption at the age of twenty-six. Charlotte Brontë again – I have been assured on good authority that Charlotte Brontë was, with the possible exception of Emily, the worst governess in the British Isles. Then there was Scott – he went bankrupt, and left, together with a few magnificent novels, one house, Abbotsford, which is perhaps the ugliest in the whole Empire. But surely these instances are enough – I need not further labour the point that highbrows, for some reason or another, are wholly incapable of dealing successfully with what is called real life. That is why, and here I come to a point that is often surprisingly ignored, they honour so wholeheartedly and depend so completely upon those who are called lowbrows. By a lowbrow is meant of course a man or a woman of thoroughbred vitality who rides his body in pursuit of a living at a gallop across life. That is why I honour and respect lowbrows – and I have never known a highbrow who did not. In so far as I am a highbrow (and my imperfections in that line are well known to me) I love lowbrows; I study them; I always sit next the conductor in an omnibus and try to get him to tell me what it is like – being a conductor. In whatever company I am I always try to know what it is like – being a conductor, being a woman with ten children and thirty-five shillings a week, being a stockbroker, being an admiral, being a bank clerk, being a dressmaker, being a duchess, being a miner, being a cook, being a prostitute. All that lowbrows do is of surpassing interest and wonder to me, because, in so far as I am a highbrow, I cannot do things myself.

This brings me to another point which is also surprisingly overlooked. Lowbrows need highbrows and honour them just as much as highbrows need lowbrows and honour them. This too is not a matter that requires much demonstration. You have only to stroll along the Strand on a wet winter's night and watch the crowds lining up to get into the movies. These lowbrows are waiting, after the day's work, in the rain, sometimes for hours, to get into the cheap seats and sit in hot theatres in order to see what their lives look like. Since they are lowbrows, engaged magnificently and adventurously in riding full tilt from one end of life to the other in pursuit of a living, they cannot see themselves doing it. Yet nothing interests them more. Nothing matters to them more. It is one of the prime necessities of life to them – to be shown what life looks like. And the highbrows, of course, are the only people who can show them. Since they are the only people who do not do things, they are the only people who can see things being done. This is so – and so it is I am certain; nevertheless we are told – the air buzzes with it by night, the press booms with it by day, the very donkeys in the fields do nothing but bray it, the very curs in the streets do nothing but bark it – 'Highbrows hate lowbrows! Lowbrows hate highbrows!' – when highbrows need lowbrows, when lowbrows need highbrows, when they cannot exist apart, when one is the complement and other side of the other! How has such a lie come into existence? Who has set this malicious gossip afloat?

There can be no doubt about that either. It is the doing of the middlebrows. They are the people, I confess, that I seldom regard with entire cordiality. They are the go-betweens; they are the busy-bodies who run from one to the other with their tittle tattle and make all the mischief – the middlebrows, I repeat. But what, you may ask, is a middlebrow? And that, to tell the truth, is no easy question to answer. They are neither one thing nor the other. They are not highbrows, whose brows are high; nor lowbrows, whose brows are low. Their brows are betwixt and between. They do not live in Bloomsbury which is on high ground; nor in Chelsea, which is on low ground. Since they must live somewhere presumably, they live perhaps in South Kensington, which is betwixt and between. The middlebrow is the man, or woman, of middlebred intelligence who ambles and saunters now on this side of the hedge, now on that, in pursuit of no single object, neither art itself nor life itself, but both mixed indistinguishably, and rather nastily, with money, fame, power, or prestige. The middlebrow curries favour with both sides equally. He goes to the lowbrows and tells them that while he is not quite one of them, he is almost their friend. Next moment he rings up the highbrows and asks them with equal geniality whether he may not come to tea. Now there are highbrows – I myself have known duchesses who were highbrows, also charwomen, and they have both told me with that vigour of language which so often unites the aristocracy with the working classes, that they would rather sit in the coal cellar, together, than in the drawing-room with middlebrows and pour out tea. I have myself been asked – but may I, for the sake of brevity, cast this scene which is only partly fictitious, into the form of fiction? – I myself, then, have been asked to come and 'see' them – how strange a passion theirs is for being 'seen'! They ring me up, therefore, at about eleven in the morning, and ask me to come to tea. I go to my wardrobe and consider, rather lugubriously, what is the right thing to wear? We highbrows may be smart, or we may be shabby; but we never have the right thing to wear. I proceed to ask next: What is the right thing to say? Which is the right knife to use? What is the right book to praise? All these are things I do not know for myself. We highbrows read what we like and do what we like and praise what we like. We also know what we dislike – for example, thin bread and butter tea. The difficulty of eating thin bread and butter in white kid gloves has always seemed to me one of life's more insuperable problems. Then I dislike bound volumes of the classics behind plate glass. Then I distrust people who call both

Shakespeare and Wordsworth equally 'Bill' – it is a habit moreover that leads to confusion. And in the matter of clothes, I like people either to dress very well; or to dress very badly; I dislike the correct thing in clothes. Then there is the question of games. Being a highbrow I do not play them. But I love watching people play who have a passion for games. These middlebrows pat balls about; they poke their bats and muff their catches at cricket. And when poor Middlebrow mounts on horseback and that animal breaks into a canter, to me there is no sadder sight in all Rotten Row. To put it in a nutshell (in order to get on with the story) that tea party was not wholly a success, nor altogether a failure; for Middlebrow, who writes, following me to the door, clapped me briskly on the back, and said 'I'm sending you my book!' (Or did he call it 'stuff'?) And his book comes – sure enough, though called, so symbolically, KEEPAWAY [Keepaway is the name of a preparation used to distract the male dog from the female at certain seasons], it comes. And I read a page here, and I read a page there (I am breakfasting, as usual, in bed). And it is not well written; nor is it badly written. It is not proper, nor is it improper – in short it is betwixt and between. Now if there is any sort of book for which I have, perhaps, an imperfect sympathy, it is the betwixt and between. And so, though I suffer from the gout of a morning – but if one's ancestors for two or three centuries have tumbled into bed dead drunk one has deserved a touch of that malady – I rise. I dress. I proceed weakly to the window. I take that book in my swollen right hand and toss it gently over the hedge into the field. The hungry sheep – did I remember to say that this part of the story takes place in the country? – the hungry sheep look up but are not fed.

But to have done with fiction and its tendency to lapse into poetry – I will now report a perfectly prosaic conversation in words of one syllable. I often ask my friends the lowbrows, over our muffins and honey, why it is that while we, the highbrows, never buy a middlebrow book, or go to a middlebrow lecture, or read, unless we are paid for doing so, a middlebrow review, they, on the contrary, take these middlebrow activities so seriously? Why, I ask (not of course on the wireless), are you so damnably modest? Do you think that a description of your lives, as they are, is too sordid and too mean to be beautiful? Is that why you prefer the middlebrow version of what they have the impudence to call real humanity? – this mixture of geniality and sentiment stuck together with a sticky slime of calves-foot jelly? The truth, if you would only believe it, is much more beautiful than any lie. Then again, I continue, how can you let the middlebrows teach you how to write? – you, who write so beautifully when you write naturally, that I would give both my hands to write as you do – for which reason I never attempt it, but do my best to learn the art of writing as a highbrow should. And again, I press on, brandishing a muffin on the point of a tea spoon, how dare the middlebrows teach you how to read – Shakespeare for instance? All you have to do is to read him. The Cambridge edition is both good and cheap. If you find HAMLET difficult, ask him to tea. He is a highbrow. Ask Ophelia to meet him. She is a lowbrow. Talk to them, as you talk to me, and you will know more about Shakespeare than all the middlebrows in the world can teach you – I do not think, by the way, from certain phrases that Shakespeare liked middlebrows, or Pope either.

To all this the lowbrows reply – but I cannot imitate their style of talking – that they consider themselves to be common people without education. It is very kind of the middlebrows to try to teach them culture. And after all, the lowbrows continue, middlebrows, like other people, have to make money. There must be money in teaching and in writing books about Shakespeare. We all have to earn our livings nowadays, my friends the lowbrows remind me. I quite agree. Even those of us whose Aunts came a cropper riding in India and left them an annual income of four hundred and fifty pounds, now reduced, thanks to the war and other luxuries, to little more than two hundred odd, even we have to do that. And we do it, too, by writing about anybody who seems amusing – enough has been written about Shakespeare – Shakespeare hardly pays. We highbrows, I agree, have to earn our livings; but when we have earned enough to live on, then we live. When the middlebrows, on the contrary, have earned enough to live on, they go on earning enough to buy – what are the things that middlebrows always buy? Queen Anne furniture (faked, but none the less expensive); first editions of dead writers, always the worst; pictures, or reproductions from pictures, by dead painters; houses in what is called 'the Georgian style' – but never anything new, never a picture by a living painter, or a chair by a living carpenter, or books by living writers, for to buy living art requires living taste. And, as that kind of art and that kind of taste are what middlebrows call 'highbrow', 'Bloomsbury', poor middlebrow spends vast sums on sham antiques, and has to keep at it scribbling away, year in, year out, while we highbrows ring each other up, and are off for a day's jaunt into the country. That is the worst of course of living in a set – one likes being with one's friends.

Have I then made my point clear, sir, that the true battle in my opinion lies not between highbrow and lowbrow, but between highbrows and lowbrows joined together in blood brotherhood against the bloodless and pernicious pest who comes between? If the BBC stood for anything but the Betwixt and Between Company they would use their control of the air not to stir strife between brothers, but to broadcast the fact that highbrows and lowbrows must band together to exterminate a pest which is the bane of all thinking and living. It may be, to quote from your advertisement columns, that 'terrifically sensitive' lady novelists overestimate the dampness and dinginess of this fungoid growth. But all I can say is that when, lapsing into that stream which people call, so oddly, consciousness, and gathering wool from the sheep that have been mentioned above, I ramble round my garden in the suburbs, middlebrow seems to me to be everywhere. 'What's that?' I cry. 'Middlebrow on the cabbages? Middlebrow infecting that poor old sheep? And what about the moon?' I look up and, behold, the moon is under eclipse. 'Middlebrow at it again!' I exclaim. 'Middlebrow obscuring, dulling, tarnishing and coarsening even the silver edge of Heaven's own scythe.' (I 'draw near to poetry', see advt.) And then my thoughts, as Freud assures us thoughts will do, rush (Middlebrow's saunter and simper, out of respect for the Censor) to sex, and I ask of the sea-gulls who are crying on desolate sea sands and of the farm hands who are coming home rather drunk to their wives, what will become of us, men and women, if Middlebrow has his way with us, and there is only a middle sex but no husbands or wives? The next remark I address with the utmost humility to the Prime Minister. 'What, sir', I demand, 'will be the fate of the British Empire and of our Dominions Across the Seas if Middlebrows prevail? Will you not, sir, read a pronouncement of an authoritative nature from Broadcasting House?'

Such are the thoughts, such are the fancies that visit 'cultured invalidish ladies with private means' (see advt.) when they stroll in their suburban gardens and look at the cabbages and at the red brick villas that have been built by middlebrows so that middlebrows may look at the view. Such are the thoughts 'at once gay and tragic and deeply feminine' (see advt.) of one who has not yet 'been driven out of Bloomsbury' (advt. again), a place where lowbrows and highbrows live happily together on equal terms and priests are not, nor priestesses, and, to be quite frank, the adjective 'priestly' is neither often heard nor held in high esteem. Such are the thoughts of one who will stay in Bloomsbury until the Duke of Bedford, rightly concerned for the respectability of his squares, raises the rent so high that Bloomsbury is safe for middlebrows to live in. Then she will leave.

> May I conclude, as I began, by thanking your reviewer for his very courteous and interesting review, but may I tell him that though he did not, for reasons best known to himself, call me a highbrow, there is no name in the world that I prefer? I ask nothing better than that all reviewers, for ever, and everywhere, should call me a highbrow. I will do my best to oblige them. If they like to add Bloomsbury, WC1, that is the correct postal address, and my telephone number is in the Directory. But if your reviewer, or any other reviewer, dares hint that I live in South Kensington, I will sue him for libel. If any human being, man, woman, dog, cat or half-crushed worm dares call me 'middlebrow' I will take my pen and stab him, dead.
>
> Yours etc.,
>
> Virginia Woolf.

Who wouldn't be afraid of Virginia Woolf in this sort of mood?

But she didn't send the letter. Writing to Ethel Smyth afterwards, she admitted that her husband had told her it would do more harm than good, and when she read it a fortnight later 'in cold blood' she could see herself in it 'as large, and ugly as could be'. 'Thanks to God, I didn't send it . . . They'd have said: she has an axe to grind; and no one would have taken me seriously.'

In her diary for 2 November, she says she has 'cellared it, against a rainy day, when I shall re-write it as an essay'. It was never published in her lifetime, but appears under the title 'Middlebrow' in the posthumous collection *The Death of the Moth and Other Essays*, published by Leonard Woolf in 1942. 'If she had lived', notes Leonard's introduction, 'there is no doubt that she would have made large alterations and revisions in nearly all these essays before allowing them to appear in volume form.' What might she have altered in this one?

'I thought it best to tell you'

Abraham Lincoln to General Meade after Gettysburg

General George Meade had just led the Union army to its first real victory in the American Civil War, but with heavy casualties on both sides. With hindsight, Meade might have finished off General Robert E. Lee's Confederate army in the days that followed the Battle of Gettysburg (3 July, 1863). But his own forces, and their supplies, were exhausted, and accurate intelligence of Confederate movements was thin on the ground. Instead of aggressively pursuing the retreating army, Meade let the bulk of it escape across the Potomac river, to the profound disappointment of President Abraham Lincoln, who had already replaced General Joseph Hooker with Meade because Hooker hadn't won the Battle of Chancellorsville a couple of months earlier.

On 14 July a pointed exchange of telegrams took place between Meade and Henry Halleck, general in chief of the Union army:

From Henry Wager Halleck to George Gordon Meade:

I need hardly say to you that the escape of Lee's army without another battle has created great dissatisfaction, in the mind of the President, and it will require an active

> and energetic pursuit on your part to remove the impression that it has not been sufficiently active heretofore.

This puts Meade in an uncomfortable double-bind: told his efforts haven't been satisfactory, yet expected to press on with enthusiasm.

> From George Gordon Meade to Henry Wager Halleck:
>
> Having performed my duty conscientiously and to the best of my ability, the censure of the President conveyed in your dispatch of 1 P. M. this day, is, in my judgment, so undeserved that I feel compelled most respectfully to ask to be immediately relieved from the command of this army.

So Meade has taken on board Lincoln's displeasure and honourably offered to resign. But then:

> From Henry Wager Halleck to George Gordon Meade:
>
> My telegram stating the disappointment of the President at the escape of Lee's army was not intended as a censure, but as a stimulus to an active pursuit. It is not deemed a sufficient cause for your application to be relieved.

It's a gloriously passive-aggressive approach that leaves Meade firmly in the wrong without giving him any chance to make amends. But in the meantime his threat to resign has gone all the way to the top, and the President drafts his own letter:

From Abraham Lincoln to George G. Meade [Draft]
Executive Mansion,
Washington, 14 July 1863.

Major General Meade

I have just seen your despatch to Gen. Halleck, asking to be relieved of your command, because of a supposed censure of mine – I am very – very – grateful to you for the magnificent success you gave the cause of the country at Gettysburg; and I am sorry now to be the author of the slightest pain to you – But I was in such deep distress myself that I could not restrain some expression of it – I had been oppressed nearly ever since the battles at Gettysburg, by what appeared to be evidences that your self, and Gen. Couch, and Gen. Smith, were not seeking a collision with the enemy, but were trying to get him across the river without another battle. What these evidences were, if you please, I hope to tell you at some time, when we shall both feel better. The case, summarily stated is this. You fought and beat the enemy at Gettysburg; and, of course, to say the least, his loss was as great as yours. He retreated; and you did not, as it seemed to me, pressingly pursue him; but a flood in the river detained him, till, by slow degrees, you were again upon him. You had at least twenty thousand veteran troops directly with you, and as many more raw ones within supporting distance, all in addition to those who fought with you at Gettysburg; while it was not possible that he had received a single recruit; and yet you stood and let the flood run down, bridges be built, and the enemy move away at his leisure, without attacking him. And Couch and Smith! The latter left Carlisle in time, upon all ordinary calculation, to have aided you in the last battle at Gettysburg; but he did not arrive. At the end of more than ten days, I believe twelve, under constant urging, he reached Hagerstown from Carlisle, which is not an inch over fifty-five miles, if so much. And Couch's movement was very little different.

Again, my dear general, I do not believe you appreciate the magnitude of the misfortune involved in Lee's escape. He was within your easy grasp, and to have closed upon him would, in connection with our other late successes, have ended the war. As it is, the war will be prolonged indefinitely. If you could not safely attack Lee last Monday, how can you possibly do so South of the river, when you can take with you very few more than two thirds of the force you then had in hand? It would be unreasonable to expect, and I do not expect you can now effect much. Your golden opportunity is gone, and I am distressed immeasurably because of it.

I beg you will not consider this a prosecution, or persecution of yourself – As you had learned that I was dissatisfied, I have thought it best to kindly tell you why.

Lincoln's explanation has the ring of an 'I'm sorry if . . .' apology, that isn't really an apology at all because it puts the blame on the other person's misunderstanding or over-sensitivity. He's backtracking frantically, but his attempts at mollifying ('I am very – very – grateful'; 'magnificent success') are simply outweighed by the reiteration of all Meade's failings and missed opportunities. It's hard not to take the accumulation of negative comments like 'such deep distress', 'the magnitude of the misfortune' and 'I was dissatisfied' as representing at least some measure of censure.

That Lincoln did not send, or even sign, the letter suggests that he realised it wasn't going to serve any useful purpose. However, writing such correspondence and storing it away unsent was to become a favourite coping mechanism for him – as it is for many of the writers in chapter IV.

Two days later, in a letter to his wife, Meade proved Lincoln's decision to hold back was probably wise:

> I wrote to you of the censure put on me by the President, through General Halleck, because I did not bag General Lee, and of the course I took on it. I don't know whether I informed you of Halleck's reply, that his telegram was not intended as a censure, but merely 'to spur me on to an active pursuit,' which I consider more offensive than the original message; for no man who does his duty, and all that he can do, as I maintain I have done, needs spurring. It is only the laggards and those who fail to do all they can do who require spurring. They have refused to relieve me, but insist on my continuing to try to do what I know in advance it is impossible to do. My army (men and animals) is exhausted; it wants rest and reorganisation; it has been greatly reduced and weakened by recent operations, and no reinforcements of any practical value have been sent. Yet, in the face of all these facts, well known to them, I am urged, pushed and spurred to attempting to pursue and destroy an army nearly equal to my own, falling back upon its resources and reinforcements, and increasing its morale daily. This has been the history of all my predecessors, and I

> clearly saw that in time their fate would be mine. This was the reason I was disinclined to take the command, and it is for this reason I would gladly give it up.

In fact, General Meade stayed in command of his army until the end of the war two years later (whereas Halleck was replaced by Ulysses E. Grant).

Resignation at the third attempt

Winston Churchill to the Prime Minister

Because the recipient only sees the final, decisive draft sent, we rarely know the hesitations and re-workings involved in the writing. Even people normally renowned for their courage and resolve may dither in private before committing themselves.

During the ill-fated Dardanelles campaign of 1915, which aimed to defeat Turkish forces at Gallipoli, Winston Churchill, who as First Lord of the Admiralty was responsible for the seaborne invasion, incessantly criticised his colleagues – including Prime Minster Asquith and War Secretary Kitchener – for what he saw as their delays and indecision over military strategy. Yet when, the expedition having ended in disaster and Churchill being made the scapegoat, he finally decided to make his point by resigning, he himself became uncharacteristically hesitant.

It took several unsent resignation letters before in November of that year he delivered one he was happy with. He had already lost his position as First Lord of the Admiralty to Balfour, following Asquith's coalition with the Tories to form a national government. He'd been relegated to the minor role of Chancellor of the Duchy of Lancaster, and knew his time in the Cabinet was up, but he must still have wanted to pick his own moment – and reasons – for going.

His first letter, drafted on 22 October, threatened to resign unless Kitchener was removed from the War Office:

> [My dear Asquith]
>
> . . . After the Cabinet the members of the War Committee remained behind to settle some points left over from our morning meeting, & Mr Balfour then informed us that he could not serve upon a Committee so small as three because of Kitchener's unsuitability to the duties of Secretary of State for War. The reasons . . . were not disputed by any one present. They are well known to you. They seem to me to apply with equal force to a Committee of five or six. There is no doubt whatever that the present Administration of the War Office does not command the confidence of any of your principal colleagues, & that a speedy change is required in the highest interests of the state . . .
>
> In these circumstances I feel it my duty to inform you that I for one cannot continue in the Government unless a change in the control of the War Office is made or is about to be made.
>
> It is with the greatest sorrow on personal grounds that I shd take leave of you. Our close friendship has never been disturbed by the political stresses & storms of nearly ten years official work at your side & under your leadership. That friendship was specially prized by me because it survived the older one wh existed between you & my father. I am sure that the course to wh I now feel bound by the strongest sense of duty & wh I must pursue no matter at what cost to myself will not impair it.

Perhaps Churchill was dissuaded from sending it by the sentiment that colours the final paragraph, or perhaps because Kitchener, although not deprived of his War Office position, was, as Roy Jenkins's Churchill biography explains, 'shipped off on a month's visit to the Dardanelles', which relieved immediate tensions in the committee. His second attempt at resignation, a week later, was more defensive, as he realised that Asquith's new, reduced war committee wouldn't have room for him.

Winston Churchill to H.H. Asquith

29 October 1915
Claridge's Hotel

My dear Asquith,

I had hoped to see you yesterday to tell [you] that our ten years work in office together must now end.

I agree with the principle of a war executive composed of the Prime Minister & the heads of the two military departments. But the change necessarily deprives me of rendering useful service.

After leaving the Admiralty five months ago I have only remained in the Government at your request in order to take part in the work of the War council. It would not be right for me at this time to remain in a sinecure. The views I have expressed on war policy are on record, and I have seen with deep regret the course which has been followed. Nor could I conscientiously accept responsibility without power. The long delays in coming to decisions have not been the only cause of our misfortunes. The faulty & lethargic execution and lack of scheme and combination over all military affairs, & of any effective concert with our Allies are evils wh will not be cured merely by the changes indicated in yr memorandum – good though these are in themselves.

I therefore take my leave of you not without many regrets on personal grounds but without any doubts. There is one point however on which it would perhaps be well for us to have a talk. It is now necessary for the truth to be made public about the initiation of the Dardanelles expedition.

It's all a little bit 'I don't want to be in your gang anyway' and, as Roy Jenkins notes, implicit in the last line, with its determination to secure his wartime reputation, is a slight hint of blackmail. Churchill wisely left this one unsent, too.

The final version, sent a fortnight after the Claridge's draft (why, you wonder, was that one written from Claridge's anyway?), is much more confident and less self-justifying:

Duchy of Lancaster Office
11 November 1915

My dear Asquith

When I left the Admiralty five months ago, I accepted an office with few duties in order at your request to take part in the work of the War Council, and to assist new Ministers with the knowledge of current operations which I then possessed in a special degree. The counsels which I have offered are upon record in the minutes of the Committee of Imperial Defence, and in the

Memoranda I have circulated to the Cabinet, and I draw your attention at the present time to these.

I am in cordial agreement with the decision to form a small War Council. I appreciated the intention you expressed to me six weeks ago to include me among its members. I foresaw then the personal difficulties which you would have to face in its composition, and I make no complaint at all that your scheme should be changed. But with that change my work in the Government comes naturally to a close.

Knowing what I do about the present situation, and the instrument of executive power, I could not accept a position of general responsibility for war policy without any effective share in its guidance & control. Even when decisions of principle are rightly taken, the speed and method of their execution are factors which determine the result. Nor do I feel able in times like these to remain in well-paid inactivity. I therefore ask you to submit my resignation to the King. I am an officer, and I place myself unreservedly at the disposal of the military authorities, observing that my regiment is in France.

I have a clear conscience which enables me to bear my responsibility for past events with composure.

Time will vindicate my administration of the Admiralty, and assign me my due share in the vast series of preparations and operations which have secured us the complete command of the seas.

With much respect, and unaltered personal friendship, I bid you goodbye.

Yours very sincerely,

Winston S. Churchill

This one was published (to acclaim) as an official statement, and followed up by a resignation speech in the House of Commons. So Churchill's instincts were right. He'd written the right letter, at the right moment, and his reputation was safe.

A week later, he arrived in France to take over a battalion of Royal Scots Fusiliers.

'Sometimes I think you don't realise . . .'

Sylvia Beach to James Joyce

Sylvia Beach was the American-born founder of the Shakespeare & Company bookshop in Paris, which specialised in British and American publications and became a gathering place for expatriate writers including Gertrude Stein, Ernest Hemingway and F. Scott Fitzgerald. In 1922 Sylvia took on the first publication, a print run of 1,000 copies, of James Joyce's *Ulysses* (which had been rejected by several established publishers), offering Joyce, according to Richard Ellmann's biography, the stupendous royalty of 66 per cent. Joyce insisted on *five* sets of proofs, and then did so much correcting and re-writing at proof stage that the text grew by a third. The printer, who was setting the type in hot metal and therefore had to re-make a page every time Joyce changed something, tore his hair out. Sylvia borrowed money in the meantime to keep her store afloat, and later helped smuggle copies of the book to readers in the United States.

Given how generous she was, lending books as well as selling them, and sometimes lending money to impoverished writers too, Joyce seems to have abused her goodwill appallingly. The slightly slapdash punctuation of this letter suggests it was written in a rush, pretty much as she thought it, and clearly in a state of extreme frustration.

12 April, 1927

Dear Mr Joyce,

I see that I owe the English publishers over two hundred pounds. The 15th is the date on which they must be paid. I have not a sufficient provision in the bank to meet all the bills and shall try to get some of the more lenient publishers to wait a fortnight, but it makes business relations very unpleasant. There are a lot of American bills too. I never try to borrow from my family. They are too poor. From what you tell me, you have only a few thousand francs left, the balance of your royalties for *Ulysses* will barely cover your rent on the 15th. You will get a big price for the manuscript of *Dubliners*, but I imagine that Rosenbach [the American collector of rare books and manuscripts] will pay only a small part of the sum down. The rest he will settle up later. Meanwhile I am afraid I and my little shop will not be able to stand the struggle to keep you and your family going from now till June, and to finance the trip of Mrs Joyce and yourself to London 'with money jingling in your pocket'. It is a very terrifying prospect for me. I already have many expenses for you that you do not dream of, and everything I have I give you freely. Sometimes I think you don't realise it, as when you said to Miss Weaver that my work was 'easing off'. The truth is that as my affection and admiration for you are unlimited, so is the work you pile on my shoulders. When you are absent, every word I receive from you is an order. The reward for my unceasing labour on your behalf is to see you tie yourself into a bowknot and hear you complain. (I am poor and tired too) and I have noticed that every time a new terrible effort is required from me, (my life is a continual 'six hours' with sprints every ten rounds) and I manage to accomplish the task that is set me you try to see how much more I can do while I am about it. Is it human?

With kindest regards

Yours very sincerely

Sylvia Beach

It deserved to be sent, so goodness knows how she restrained herself. By 1931 (again, according to Ellmann) Joyce was receiving 12,000 francs (£94) a month in royalties from *Ulysses*, but still failing to live within his income and regularly asking Sylvia for more. (Later the book sold to Random House in New York for a $45,000 advance, of which he never offered her a penny.)

Publishing the book nearly ruined her, although she did manage to keep the shop going until the Second World War, when it was closed by the German occupation. In 1951 a new establishment was opened under the same name by George Whitman, an admiring American GI stationed in Paris during the war, and is still run by his daughter, whom he named after her: Sylvia Beach Whitman. In tribute to the original Sylvia and the principles on which Shakespeare & Company was founded, George's shop offered – and still offers – free lodging to writers in return for their help in the store.

You can only hope they're more appreciative than Joyce was.

'My reason has half foundered'

Van Gogh's last-but-one letter to his brother

Vincent Van Gogh, the manic-Impressionist Dutch painter of sunflowers and haystacks, who only sold one painting during his lifetime and famously cut off his own ear and delivered part of it to a girlfriend, finally lost his lust for life at the age of 37. By this time he was living in the village of Auvers-sur-Oise in northern France, and relying on the financial, and emotional, support of his younger brother Theo, an art dealer. He visited Theo and his family in Paris in early July 1890 and, back in Auvers, wrote in mid-month hoping to return soon, with some large canvases of wheat fields which he felt 'will tell you what I can't say in words, what I consider healthy and fortifying about the countryside'. It clearly wasn't fortifying enough, because by the end of the month Vincent was dead.

In the last couple of weeks of his life he wrote two letters to Theo and his wife Johanna – but only one of them was sent.

The last letter Theo received from him, dated 23 July, tries hard to be upbeat, talking about the vigour with which he is applying himself to his work ('I am trying to do as well as certain painters whom I have greatly loved'), and the enjoyment he gets from artists he admires ('I noticed with pleasure that the Gauguin from Brittany which I saw was very beautiful'). Vincent seems practical and forward-looking, enclosing a sketch of his own that he's pleased with, making requests for materials, both for himself and for a fellow artist, and even discussing arrangements for the payment (although he keeps his own order to a minimum, perhaps a hint that he won't need art materials for much longer?). But there's something uncomfortable about his sign-off: 'Good-by now, and good luck in business, etc., remember me to Jo and hand-shakes in thought.' That bracing 'hand-shake', as though he doesn't want his brother to know his mental distress . . .

Vincent shot himself in the chest on 27 July, and died from the wound on the 29th. The note found on his body is sometimes described as his final letter, but is so similar to the one dated the 23rd that it feels far more like a first draft. Either that, or the words of the first were still echoing in his head and he forgot he'd already written them down.

Both letters begin by thanking Theo for a 50-franc hand-out, and both describe how hard it is to put what he wants to say into words. But the unsent letter has no attempt at positivity. It's as though, realising how despairing and gloomy it sounded, he then re-wrote it inserting as many happier comments as possible. Read the unsent letter, here, and the tone of that other ending – 'good luck, hand-shakes in thought' – suddenly feels more ominous.

My dear brother,

Thanks for your kind letter and for the 50-fr. note it contained.

There are many things I should like to write you about, but I feel it is useless. I hope you have found those worthy gentlemen favourably disposed toward you.

Your reassuring me as to the peacefulness of your

household was hardly worth the trouble, I think, having seen the weal and woe of it for myself. And I quite agree with you that rearing a boy on a fourth floor is a hell of a job for you as well as for Jo.

Since the thing that matters most is going well, why should I say more about things of less importance?
My word, before we have a chance to talk business more collectedly, we shall probably have a long way to go.

The other painters, whatever they think, instinctively keep themselves at a distance from discussions about the actual trade.

Well, the truth is, we can only make our pictures speak. But yet, my dear brother, there is this that I have always told you, and I repeat it once more with all the earnestness that can be expressed by the effort of a mind diligently fixed on trying to do as well as possible – I tell you again that I shall always consider you to be something more than a simple dealer in Corots, that through my mediation you have your part in the actual production of some canvases, which will retain their calm even in the catastrophe.

For this is what we have got to, and this is all or at least the main thing that I can have to tell you at a moment of comparative crisis. At a moment when things are very strained between dealers in pictures of dead artists, and living artists.

Well, my own work, I am risking my life for it and my reason has half foundered because of it – that's all right – but you are not among the dealers in men as far as I know, and you can still choose your side, I think, acting with humanity, but que veux-tu?

It's not so obviously suicidal that Theo would have realised any immediate danger, but the references to 'catastrophe', 'crisis' and risks to life and reason might have sounded a warning bell . . .

And another thing . . .

David O. Selznick to Alfred Hitchcock

The Hollywood film producer David Selznick, the man who brought us *Gone With the Wind*, was renowned for firing off heated memos haranguing studio heads, directors, scriptwriters and movie staff.

The filming of Daphne du Maurier's *Rebecca* in 1939, which Alfred Hitchcock was hired to direct, was the cause of many of them, beset as it was by problems of casting and scripting even before the cameras started rolling. Selznick had had to fight for the casting of Joan Fontaine in the role of the Girl (over Anne Baxter, Vivien Leigh and Loretta Young) because nobody else considered her talented enough, but he believed she'd be OK with Hitchcock's direction. He wanted to replicate the massive success of the book by staying faithful to it on film, but also had to get it past the censors, which is why Laurence Olivier's Maxim de Winter, as the hero, is not allowed to have killed his wife deliberately, as in the novel.

Hitchcock's original treatment had already provoked a series of memos complaining about changes to plot and character. One, dated 12 June 1939, which Selznick himself admits is a 'lecture', begins: 'Dear Hitch, It is my unfortunate and distressing task to tell you that I am disappointed beyond words by the treatment of *Rebecca*.'

By September, following the outbreak of war, he was working to extra financial and time constraints. This memo shows Selznick's fuse getting shorter as his list of complaints grows longer – and more convoluted. The second paragraph, in particular, reminds me of how Humphrey Lyttelton used to introduce the One Song to the Tune of Another round in Radio 4's *I'm Sorry I Haven't a Clue*, where the explanation of the rules takes almost as long as the game itself . . .

September 19, 1939
To: Mr. Hitchcock

Dear Hitch:

I am putting this in writing because there seems to be some difficulty on the part of Henry [Ginsberg] and the Production Department in making our complaints clear, and I want there to be no misunderstanding of any steps if they eventually become necessary because of your failure, or (and I dislike to think this) your refusal, to understand what it is that we are complaining about . . .

Cutting your film with the camera and reducing the number of angles required is highly desirable, and no one appreciates its value more than I do; but certainly it is of no value if you are simply going to give us less cut film per day than a man who shoots twice as many angles. Eliminating additional angles without eliminating the time that is spent on these additional angles, and actually through increasing the time that would be spent by other men if they secured these additional angles, is no feat. As somebody said the other day, 'Hitchcock shoots like

Van Dyke – except that he gets one third as much film,' which means that you cut your film with your camera the way Van Dyke does but that he gets three times as much cut film per day.

I am aware that it takes time to get the performance out of Joan Fontaine, but every picture I have ever worked on had some such difficulty, and you are fortunate in having a completely competent cast of highly expert actors . . . Miss Fontaine . . . requires work – but so has every other girl who has been aimed at stardom and who requires an enormous amount of work in her first big opportunity. Your difficulties in shooting this picture are a great deal less than the difficulties on the usual picture. And in most studios you wouldn't have anything like the cast you have now: you would have a great deal cheaper actors, and would have great difficulties with a great many of your roles . . . and you would be expected to make about twice the time you are making.

Nor do I feel that the condition of the script is even a factor. I will not go into the fact that the condition of the script is in my opinion largely due to your reluctance to do a more faithful job on scenes from the book, despite my pleas that you should do so over a period of months. Perhaps you can charge me with the condition of the script. But whether you or I is responsible, or we are responsible jointly (which is probably nearer to the truth), does not dismiss the fact that on every scene that you have made you have had the script many days ahead and there has been no question of it coming out at the last minute. Actually, the script of each scene on this picture has in every case been out very much earlier than on almost any picture we have ever made, including *Gone With the Wind*, *A Star Is Born*, *The Prisoner of Zenda*, etc. And there are some good directors in this town who, for some reason unknown to me, persist in having each scene rewritten after it is rehearsed on the stage, and who still manage to make infinitely better time than we are making on *Rebecca*.

This complaint would have been identical a month or six weeks ago. Today, when we are faced with the probability of a large loss on *Rebecca* because of war conditions, it is no longer a matter of better time being desirable, it is a necessity. In all other studios in town producers and directors are trying to figure out how they can cut down their normal shooting schedules and budgets by 25 to 50 per cent. And their normal schedules and budgets are a great deal higher than what we have been hoping for on *Rebecca*. Good average time on *Rebecca* would be acceptable in normal conditions, although regrettable today; bad time on *Rebecca*, regrettable and untenable as it might be in normal times, is impossible of acceptance today.

There are various things about your methods of shooting which I think you simply must correct, because even if we permitted you to follow them on *Rebecca*, you would have to cure them on your next picture and succeeding pictures because nobody in Hollywood would stand for them, so we might as well clamp down on you for this picture. I refer to such things as letting the actors remain idle while the camera crew lines up, and the camera crew remain idle while the actors are being rehearsed. It is just infantile not to realise that these two processes must go through simultaneously, and if the noise disturbs you, then rehearse them on the sidelines or somewhere.

God knows that this studio has never been famous for its speed of production. In fact, our pictures have always been made more slowly than comparable pictures in almost any other studio in town. We had hoped to correct this on *Rebecca*. Instead, we find that we are behind even normal-prosperity-time speed . . .

I know that you are working late evenings, but working late means overtime and overtime means additional cost – and these additional hours in the evening are only justified to improve normal shooting time. They are certainly not justified to make up shooting time that has been wasted in the course of the day, particularly when these extra hours don't even make up for the lost time. We want these extra hours, although they perhaps might not be necessary if we had achieved real John Ford type of speed in the course of the day; but we want them, in addition, to do a good full day's work and not as an inadequate and expensive substitute for it.

. . . My fondness for you personally, and my respect for your abilities, cannot blind me to my responsibility to the people who are financing these pictures, and to the employees whose jobs depend upon efficient shooting on the stage . . .

I will be very happy to discuss with you tonight at the studio, or at my home, or over a drink, or tomorrow, or any other time. Or, if you wish, we will say no more about it and just look to a difference in result.

DOS

It was never sent – perhaps because Selznick realised Hitchcock was a law unto himself. His wife Irene often persuaded him to wait and re-consider his memos before sending them (preventing his own resignation at least once), but Hitch must have pulled up his socks anyway, because *Rebecca* went on to win two Oscars, including Best Picture, and nine more nominations, including one for Joan Fontaine as Best Actress. So Selznick's instincts were proved right – although Hitchcock did much for her realistically terrified, insecure performance by constantly telling her the rest of the cast didn't like her, and on one occasion slapping her to produce the tears the scene required.

Hitchcock himself, incidentally, enjoyed using unsent letters as a device in his films. In *Suspicion*, Lina Aysgarth (Joan Fontaine again) writes a note telling her charming but fraudulent husband Johnnie (Cary Grant) that she is leaving him, having discovered yet another instance of his dishonesty, but changes her mind and tears it up on hearing news of her father's sudden death, distraught at the prospect of enduring another loss. (Hitchcock allegedly wanted to end the film with Lina, having realised that Johnnie is a murderer, writing a letter to her mother exposing his guilt, and giving it to Johnnie himself to post before drinking the glass of milk she knows he has poisoned. Which would have been brilliant – a sort of virtual, posthumous, sending of the crucial letter – but of course Hitchcock wasn't allowed to cast Cary Grant as a cold-hearted killer, so the film ending is left ambiguous.)

And in *Vertigo*, Judy Barton, unwilling accomplice in a murder plot, writes a letter of confession (also providing an exposition for the audience) to the detective she's in love with, who doesn't yet realise her involvement in the crime. Planning to leave town, she writes, 'If I had the nerve I'd stay and lie, hoping that I could make you love me again . . . But I don't know whether I have the nerve to try.' At which point she decides to have a go at it anyway, ripping up the note before going out to dinner with him and embarking on a new round of deception.

'Nothing here to eat except omelettes and oranges and onions'

Katherine Mansfield to Frederick Goodyear

In a 1950 letter to his long-term companion Monica Jones, the poet Philip Larkin refers to a letter of hers which he says 'put me faintly in mind of one K.M. wrote to a young man called Goodyear . . . but charitably left unposted'.

What, you can't help wondering, was in that letter from Katherine Mansfield?

It turns out to have been written in March 1916. Frederick Goodyear, a friend of the New Zealand-born writer and her lover (later husband) John Middleton Murry, was at this point serving at the Front, with the Meteorological Office of the Royal Engineers, and had a few weeks earlier written *her* a letter that ended: 'If love is only love when it is resistless, I don't love you. But if it is a relative emotion, I do. Personally, I think everything everywhere is bunkum.' Katherine's response (with its oddly random use of apostrophes) is marked in her *Collected Letters* as an 'autograph draft'. Although the introduction admits that it's usually impossible to establish whether the drafts found in her notebooks were sent or not, Larkin seems convinced it wasn't, and you can see why he hoped not.

4 March 1916

Villa Pauline, Bandol

Mr F.G.

Never did cowcumber lie more heavy on a female's buzzum than your curdling effugion which I have read twice and wont again if horses drag me. But I keep wondering, and cant for the life of me think, whatever there was in mine to so importantly disturb you. (Henry James is dead. Did you know?) I did not, swayed by a resistless passion say that I loved you . . . And why should you write to me as though I'd got into the family way with H.G.W[ells] and driven round to you in a hansom cab to ask you to make a respectable woman of me? Yes, youre bad tempered, suspicious and surly. And if you think I flung my bonnet over you as a possible mill, my lad, you're mistook.

In fact, now I come to ponder on your last letter I don't believe you want to write to me at all and Im hanged if Ill shoot arrows in the air. But perhaps that is temper on my part; it is certainly pure stomach. Im so hungry, simply empty, and seeing in my minds eye just now a sirloin of beef, well browned with plenty of gravy *and* horseradish sauce and baked potatoes I nearly sobbed. There's nothing here to eat except omelettes and oranges and onions. Its a cold, sunny windy day – the kind of day when you want a tremendous feed for lunch & an armchair in front of the fire to boaconstrict in afterwards. I feel sentimental about England now – English food, *decent* English *waste*! How much better than these thrifty french whose flower gardens are nothing but potential salad bowls. There's not a leaf in

France that you cant 'faire une infusion avec', not a blade that isn't bon pour la cuisine. By God, Id like to buy a pound of the best butter, put it on the window sill and watch it melt to spite em. They are a stingy uncomfortable crew for all their lively scrapings . . . For instance, in their houses – what appalling furniture – and never one comfortable chair. If you want to talk the only possible thing to do is go to bed. Its a case of either standing on your feet or lying in comfort under a puffed up eiderdown. I quite understand the reason for what is called french moral laxity – you're simply forced into bed – no matter with whom – there's no other place for you. . . Supposing a *young* man comes to see about the electric light & will go on talking and pointing to the ceiling, or a friend drops in to tea and asks you if you believe in Absolute Evil. How can you give your mind to these things when youre sitting on four knobs and a square inch of cane. How much better to lie snug and *give yourself up to it.*

Later.
Now I've eaten one of the omelettes and one of the oranges. The sun has gone in; its beginning to thunder. There's a little bird on a tree outside this window not so much singing as sharpening a note – He's getting a very fine point on it; I expect you would know his name . . . Write to me again when everything is not *too* bunkum.

Goodbye for now

With my 'strictly relative' love

'K.M'

It would have been worth receiving just for the idea of 'boaconstricting' a huge lunch, so I'm rather sorry that Goodyear never got it (if he really didn't). But you can perhaps imagine Larkin being appalled at Mansfield fantasising about food and furniture in the middle of what her recipient had hoped would be a love letter – and while he was presumably enduring rather more hunger and discomfort on the Western Front. She was obviously fond of Goodyear, though, as his letters were among the few, apart from Murry's, that she kept. He died the following year, after being wounded during an attack near Arras.

IV

Letters As Therapy

These days, the story of Abraham Lincoln's unsent letter to General Meade after Gettysburg turns up everywhere, from management training to personal improvement and church teaching. Dale Carnegie quotes it in his 1936 bestselling business bible *How to Win Friends and Influence People,* as an example of getting your emotions out of the way so that reason can be reasserted and wise decisions made. I even found it posted on the Daily Devotions page of an online gospel site called the Lutheran Hour Ministries: 'Whenever Abraham Lincoln had to *vent* at someone's foolishness or wrongness, he put all of his feelings into a *hot letter,*' says the pastor. 'Then he would take that letter and put it aside.' What started by accident has been developed into a full-blown self-help strategy, along the lines of 'What would Lincoln do?'

So why not cut out the recipient and just do the venting? All those books with titles like *Write It Down and Let It Go*; the proliferation of websites that encourage an outpouring of rage or grief; the online projects where you can upload the thoughts you'd like to send; the personal development techniques that urge you to express your feelings in a safe space: they all tell us that it's good to write, that we don't actually need to send our letter. Just putting it all down will clarify our thoughts and set us free, without having to confront difficult people or jeopardise fragile relationships by addressing them in real life.

It's especially good advice for the broken-hearted: write to your ex, but don't send the letter. The lyrics of Alanis Morrisette's 1998 song 'Unsent' are composed entirely as letters to former friends and lovers – self-destructive Jonathan, the Terrance she loved muchly, and the rest of them. The moral, always with exes, is don't send: you can't go back. Write it to yourself instead.

Some experts actually advise *sending* it to yourself – a sort of virtual sending with no consequences (except that you get to experience what it would feel like to be on the receiving end, which is a useful exercise in itself). Or that you write it and then have a ceremonial burning.

But you could just throw it away. Or file it as a record of your own contemporaneous thoughts – like President Truman did on a regular basis (although in his case not writing about former lovers). It's reassuring to know that the instinct to vent has a rational, common-sense explanation behind it, and that it's a strategy favoured by the great and the good as well as the stuff of self-help manuals.

The *Guardian* even has its own regular 'A Letter To' column, where readers can give voice to their feelings about exes, friends, estranged siblings, dead parents: to the mistress a husband doesn't realise his wife knows about, to the unnamed person who was rude to you last week on the bus. (Although some of these are edging suspiciously close to 'sent' letter territory. You might be living dangerously if you let off steam by making your thoughts public in a newspaper or on a website, even anonymously, and it rather undermines the idea of 'letting it go' if you entertain a sneaking hope that your ex-lover or disloyal friend will see it.)

At its purest and most potent, the therapy letter provides relief by addressing a specific person about a specific problem – you may even envisage every word striking home like pins in a voodoo doll. But venting your feelings safe in the knowledge that they won't actually be heard means you can write letters to whoever you want, about whatever you want.

And from there, it's only a small step to addressing someone famous – someone powerful enough to soothe all woes, but distant enough to maintain your anonymity for all time. You can rant at a variety of people – living politicians and dead philosophers, like Moses Herzog in Saul Bellow's novel – or confide in a single person, if you can convince yourself you've got a sympathetic listener. You might call that prayer: in Willy Russell's 2000 novel *The Wrong Boy*, 19-year-old Raymond Marks tries to makes sense of his life by writing long, self-analytical letters to his own personal God, Morrissey of the Smiths.

Either way, the advantage of having a fantasy recipient for your unsent letter is that they're always there, and they won't interrupt or get worn down by sympathy fatigue.

'You write just like the usual egghead'

All the letters Harry S. Truman never mailed

'Give 'em Hell Harry' (the name President Harry S. Truman acquired for his outspoken style on the campaign trail) took over at the White House on the death of Roosevelt in 1945, but won a second term in 1948 on his own merits, confounding the polls to beat Thomas Dewey, the Republican Governor of New York. And he gave his correspondents hell on paper, too, writing forthright letters to let off steam. Hundreds of these were never sent – just venting his rage was enough to calm him down – but Truman was scrupulous about keeping them nonetheless. In fact, there's a whole book devoted to them: *Strictly Personal and Confidential (The Letters Harry Truman Never Mailed,* edited by Monte M. Poen). That's the biggest irony: he was too short-tempered to stop himself banging out these impetuous rants, yet his ability to see the long view and his reverence for well-documented history led him to preserve every single one he didn't send. (President Trump, of course, also preserves his off-the-cuff, 6 a.m. first drafts for posterity – but he does it by sending them to the entire world via Twitter.)

One correspondent given short shrift by Truman was the pastor of a Kansas City Methodist church. The Reverend Raymond B. Kimbrell wrote to the President criticising his political loyalties and economic policy, declaring that the US could no longer count on an 1849-style Gold Rush to save it from economic collapse (America was in the middle of a post-war recession that lasted from November 1948 to October 1949). He also objected to Truman's intemperate language and scolded him for 'cussing in public'. A favourite epithet of Truman's when referring to opponents was 'son of a bitch' – in the light of which, the pastor should have counted himself lucky to receive a brief, cordial reply from the White House; Truman's original version, below, was safely filed away.

April 12, 1949
My dear Mr Kimbrell:

Your typewritten note to me opening with 'Dear Harry,' is most interesting. I do not know you well enough to say 'Dear Ray' to you.

The President of the United States appreciates your interest in his welfare. I am delighted as an individual to call your attention to Daniel Chapter 3 verses 47 to 49 inclusive, Esther Chapters 5 and 6, and to Matthew Chapter 26 verses 47 to 49 inclusive. All these references have to do with loyalty both to God and to people. I am somewhat surprised that a good Methodist preacher – if you are a good one – would advise the Chief Executive of this great Republic to become a double crosser. For your information, I have been and am being a successful President. The people think that too, as conclusively proved Nov. 2 '48.

The only Congress I ever damned was one that needed more than that. It was the 80th, probably with one exception, the worst in our history. [This sat from 3 January

1947 to 3 January 1949: it had a Republican majority and Truman nicknamed it the 'do-nothing Congress'.]

If gold in 1849 had any effect on the panic of 1873 I fail to see the connection.

Public use of emphatic language, in certain cases, is a prerogative the President will never forego. Your judgment of what makes a bigger and better man is about on a par with Horace Greeley's, old Medill McCormack's, Hearst's and James Gordon Bennett's. You should look them up. The *Kansas City Star*, Pearson, *Life*, *Time*, Winchell and maybe Fulton Lewis are your authorities, I presume.

Best of luck to you and may you eventually become a tolerant, honest, good religious leader.

Sincerely,

Truman knew his Bible – he claimed to have read it right through twice by the age 12, the large print making it the easiest book in the house for his poor eyesight to deal with – so it may not have been wise of the Reverend Kimbrell to mess with him.

As for the cussing in public, Kimbrell probably didn't know the half of it. On one notable occasion, when Truman had described something as 'Republican horse manure', and an aide suggested to his wife that she might get him to tone down his language, she replied, 'You don't know how many years it's taken me to get him to say manure.'

He was equally brusque in dealing with those (in this case a military historian) who questioned his decision to drop the atomic bomb on Hiroshima and Nagasaki.

[Late April 1962]

My dear Mr Feis:

You write just like the usual egghead. The facts are before you but you'd like to garble them. The instruction of July 25th, 1945 was final. It was made by the Commander in Chief after Japan refused to surrender.

Churchill, Stimson, Patterson, Eisenhower and all the rest agreed that it had to be done. It was. It ended the Jap War. That was the objective. Now if you can think of any other, 'if, as, and when' egghead contemplations, bring them out.

You get the same answer – to end the Jap War and save ¼ of a million of our youngsters and that many Japs from death and twice that many on each side from being maimed for life.

It is a great thing that you or any other contemplator 'after the fact' didn't have to make the decision.

Our boys would all be dead.

Even Eleanor Roosevelt, his predecessor's widow and an international heroine in her own right, got short shrift from Truman – a veteran of the Battle of Meuse-Argonne on the Western Front – when after the war she attempted to intercede on behalf of conscientious objectors who had been imprisoned for draft-dodging.

May 17, 1948

Dear Mrs. Roosevelt

I read your letter of thirteenth with a great deal of interest. I have thoroughly looked into the conscientious objectors case and, I think, all the honest conscientious objectors have been released.

I'll admit that it is rather difficult for me to look on a conscientious objector with patience while your four sons and my three nephews were risking their lives to save our Government, and the things for which we stand, these people were virtually shooting them in the back.

I ran across one conscientious objector that I really believe is all man – he was a young Naval Pharmacist Mate who served on Okinawa carrying wounded sailors and marines from the battle field. I decorated him with a Congressional Medal of Honor. I asked him how it came about that he as a conscientious objector was willing to go into the things of the battlefield and he said to me that he could serve the Lord and save lives as well there as anywhere else in the world. He didn't weigh over one hundred and forty pounds and he was about five feet six inches tall. I shall never forget him.

My experience in the first world war with conscientious objectors was not a happy one – the majority of those with whom I came in contact were just plain cowards and shirkers – that is the reason I asked Justice Roberts to make a complete survey of the situation and to release all those that he felt were honestly conscientious objectors and that has been done.

My sympathies with the rest of them are not very strong, as you can see. I do appreciate your interest in them and can see now that all danger is passed why they would want to get out of jail.

Sincerely yours,

'I should have shaken you out of my life'

Oscar Wilde to Lord Alfred Douglas

By the time Oscar Wilde wrote *De Profundis*, his long, impassioned account of the time he served in Reading Gaol for 'gross indecency' (the worst case, said the judge, that he had ever tried), he had been in prison for over a year, his world reduced from a five-storey house in Chelsea to a 13ft x 7ft cell. He'd exchanged a life of hedonism and beauty for one of restriction, ugliness and brutally hard labour – literally, up to six hours a day on the prison treadmill. No wonder he needed someone to rant at. But we wouldn't have the text of *De Profundis* at all if it hadn't been written in the form of a letter – to Lord Alfred Douglas (Bosie), the former lover he blamed for his incarceration in the first place. Douglas had goaded Wilde into bringing a libel case against his father, the 9th Marquess of Queensberry, with the result that his homosexual liaisons were dragged into court and the prosecution was directed against him instead.

It's unlikely that prison regulations would have allowed him to compose plays or poems from his cell, but there was nothing to stop him writing a letter, and because it was still unfinished at the end of each day, it was simply returned to him (by the enlightened, liberal new prison governor James Nelson, who also kept him supplied with paper and pens) to be continued the following morning. And so on, for three months, from January to March 1897. Instead of being inspected, as prisoners' letters normally were before sending, it remained his own property. And because it stayed unsent for so long, it evolved from its initial recriminatory outburst against Lord Alfred and his family into a full-blown philosophical essay and a soul-baring analysis of his own life and nature.

The start is straightforward enough, reproaching Douglas for not having written to him, which must have been doubly painful in a place where letters ('the little messengers between me and that beautiful world of Art where once I was King') meant so much to him.

> To Lord Alfred Douglas
>
> HM Prison, Reading
>
> Dear Bosie,
>
> After long and fruitless waiting I have determined to write to you myself, as much for your sake as for mine, as I would not like to think that I had passed through two long years of imprisonment without ever having received a single line from you, or any news or message even, except such as gave me pain . . .

At times he rages like we all do when trying to make sense of conflicted emotions over a difficult relationship, bewailing his own part in the catastrophe as well as blaming Douglas, sometimes unfairly. 'Of course I should have got rid of you. I should have shaken you out of my life as a man shakes from his raiment a thing that has stung him . . . I blame myself again for having allowed you to bring me to utter and discreditable financial ruin.' At others, he drives himself mad with the injustice of the situation. 'I could not apologise to your father for his having insulted me and persecuted me in the most loathsome manner . . . You were the only person who could have done anything.'

But gradually the personal anger mutates into a more philosophical tone, so that it starts to feel like a session on the psychiatrist's couch as he tries to understand the problems that corroded his relationship with Douglas: 'Hate blinds people. You were not aware of that. Love can read the writing on the remotest star, but Hate so blinded you that you could see no further than the narrow, walled-in, and already lust-withered garden of your common desires.' And he wants Douglas to understand, too – to pass on what he is discovering during his enforced stay on the couch: 'Are you beginning now to understand a little? Is your imagination wakening from the long lethargy in which it has lain?'

The effect is cathartic and transformative, as he realises that blaming Douglas is doing him no good. 'And the end of it all is that I have got to forgive you. I must do so. I don't write this letter to put bitterness into your heart, but to pluck it out of mine. For my own sake I must forgive you.' This is the moment when the 'therapy' really kicks in: from this comment on, for the next 30-odd pages, he no longer rails at Douglas – in fact barely addresses him at all (except to say, now and then, something to the effect of 'Are you following this?'). Instead he embarks on a long journey of self-examination, exploring his own faults and downfall.

> The gods had given me almost everything. I had genius, a distinguished name, high social position, brilliancy, intellectual daring: I made art a philosophy, and philosophy an art: I altered the minds of men and the colours of things: there was nothing I said or did that did not make people wonder: I took the drama, the most objective form known to art, and made it as personal a mode of expression as the lyric or the sonnet, at the same time that I widened its range and enriched its characterisation: drama, novel, poem in rhyme, poem in prose, subtle or fantastic dialogue, whatever I touched I made beautiful in a new mode of beauty: to truth itself I gave what is false no less than what is true as its rightful province, and showed that the false and the true are merely forms of intellectual existence. I treated Art as the supreme reality, and life as a mere mode of fiction: I awoke the imagination of my century so that it created myth and legend around me: I summed up all systems in a phrase, and all existence in an epigram.

All of which might seem a vainglorious, trumpet-blowing assessment of his achievements, if he didn't follow it with:

> Along with these things . . . I let myself be lured into long spells of senseless and sensual ease. I amused myself with being a *flâneur*, a dandy, a man of fashion. I surrounded myself with the smaller natures and the meaner minds. I became the spendthrift of my own genius, and to waste an eternal youth gave me a curious joy. Tired of being on the heights, I deliberately went to the depths in the search for new sensation. What the paradox was to me in the

sphere of thought, perversity became to me in the sphere of passion. Desire, at the end, was a malady, or a madness, or both. I grew careless of the lives of others. I took pleasure where it pleased me and passed on. I forgot that every little action of the common day makes or unmakes character, and that therefore what one has done in the secret chamber one has some day to cry aloud on the housetops. I ceased to be Lord over myself. I was no longer the Captain of my Soul, and did not know it. I allowed you to dominate me, and your father to frighten me. I ended in horrible disgrace. There is only one thing for me now, absolute Humility: just as there is only one thing for you, absolute Humility also. You had better come down into the dust and learn it beside me.

I have lain in prison for nearly two years. Out of my nature has come wild despair; an abandonment to grief that was piteous even to look at; terrible and impotent rage; bitterness and scorn; anguish that wept aloud; misery that could find no voice; sorrow that was dumb. I have passed through every possible mood of suffering. Better than Wordsworth himself I know what Wordsworth meant when he said—

'Suffering is permanent, obscure, and dark
And has the nature of Infinity.'

But while there were times when I rejoiced in the idea that my sufferings were to be endless, I could not bear them to be without meaning. Now I find hidden away in my nature something that tells me that nothing in the whole world is meaningless, and suffering least of all. That something hidden away in my nature, like a treasure in a field, is Humility.

It is the last thing left in me, and the best: the ultimate discovery at which I have arrived: the starting-point for a fresh development. It has come to me right out of myself, so I know that it has come at the proper time. It could not have come before, nor later. Had any one told me of it, I would have rejected it. Had it been brought to me, I would have refused it. As I found it, I want to keep it. I must do so. It is the one thing that has in it the elements of life, of a new life, *Vita Nuova* for me. Of all things it is the strangest. One cannot acquire it, except by surrendering everything that one has. It is only when one has lost all things, that one knows that one possesses it.

Now I have realised that it is in me, I see quite clearly what I have got to do, what, in fact, I must do. And when I use such a phrase as that, I need not tell you that I am not alluding to any external sanction or command. I admit none. I am far more of an individualist than I ever was. Nothing seems to me of the smallest value except what one gets out of oneself. My nature is seeking a fresh mode of self-realisation. That is all I am concerned with. And the first thing that I have got to do is to free myself from any possible bitterness of feeling against you.

I am completely penniless, and absolutely homeless. Yet there are worse things in the world than that. I am quite candid when I tell you that rather than go out from this prison with bitterness in my heart against you or against the world I would gladly and readily beg my bread from door to door. If I got nothing from the house of the rich, I would get something at the house of the poor. Those who have much are often greedy. Those who have

> little always share. I would not a bit mind sleeping in the cool grass in summer, and when winter came on sheltering myself by the warm close-thatched rick, or under the penthouse of a great barn, provided I had love in my heart. The external things of life seem to me now of no importance at all . . .
>
> The supreme vice is shallowness. Whatever is realised is right.
>
> When first I was put into prison some people advised me to try and forget who I was. It was ruinous advice. It is only by realising what I am that I have found comfort of any kind. Now I am advised by others to try on my release to forget that I have ever been in a prison at all. I know that would be equally fatal. It would mean that I would always be haunted by an intolerable sense of disgrace, and that those things that are meant as much for me as for anybody else – the beauty of the sun and moon, the pageant of the seasons, the music of daybreak and the silence of great nights, the rain falling through the leaves, or the dew creeping over the grass and making it silver – would all be tainted for me, and lose their healing power, and their power of communicating joy. To regret one's own experiences is to arrest one's own development. To deny one's own experiences is to put a lie into the lips of one's own life. It is no less than a denial of the Soul.

The man who had turned flippancy into an art form has discovered seriousness.

Wilde analyses himself very effectively when he recalls having confined himself to

> the sunlit side of the garden, and shunned the other side for its shadow and its gloom. Failure, disgrace, poverty, sorrow, despair, suffering, tears even, the broken words that come from lips in pain, remorse that makes one walk on thorns, conscience that condemns, self-abasement that punishes, the misery that puts ashes on its head, the anguish that chooses sack-cloth for its raiment and into its own drink puts gall – all these were things of which I was afraid. And as I had determined to know nothing of them, I was forced to taste each of them in turn, to feed on them, to have for a season, indeed, no other food at all.

The ending of the letter shows him making peace with both himself and with Douglas, and looking forward with confidence:

> What seemed to the world and to myself my future I lost irretrievably when I let myself be taunted into taking the action against your father: had, I dare say, lost it really long before that. What lies before me is my past. I have got to make myself look on that with different eyes, to make the world look on it with different eyes, to make God look on it with different eyes. This I cannot do by ignoring it, or slighting it, or praising it, or denying it. It is only to be done by fully accepting it as an inevitable part of the evolution of my life and character: by bowing my head to everything that I have suffered. How far I am away from the true temper of soul, this letter in its changing, uncertain moods, its scorn and bitterness, its aspirations and its failure to realise those aspirations, shows you quite clearly. But do not forget in what a

terrible school I am sitting at my task. And incomplete, imperfect, as I am, yet from me you may have still much to gain. You came to me to learn the Pleasure of Life and the Pleasure of Art. Perhaps I am chosen to teach you something much more wonderful, the meaning of Sorrow, and its beauty. Your affectionate friend.

Oscar Wilde

He left Reading with the letter on 19 May 1897, more than 50,000 words on thin blue prison paper, and took it with him to Dieppe, where he gave it to his friend Robert Ross with instructions for it to be sent to Douglas. So it was sent in the end, although Douglas always insisted that he burned it without reading it. Like many of the letters we write in extreme emotion, it may have seemed to Wilde less significant once he was free – the pain of its most bitter passages seems to have been forgotten, enough at least for Wilde and Douglas to attempt to live together in France and Italy, and Wilde died a couple of years later, aged only 46, with all those good intentions unfulfilled (although he did convert to Catholicism on his deathbed).

The 1905 edition of the letter published by Robert Ross as *De Profundis* omits all reference to Douglas, and reads like a public apology, a declaration to the world that he has learned his lesson. It's only when you read the full, original text that you understand what was driving him, and it's the fact that the letter was unsent for so long that made it what it was. If he'd sent Douglas his thoughts straight away they wouldn't have evolved into something so far-reaching. And we wouldn't have known that love can read the writing on the remotest star.

Writing letters to everyone under the sun

Saul Bellow's *Herzog*

Like Oscar Wilde, the protagonist of Bellow's 1964 novel has hit a crisis in his life and is trying to making peace with himself. It's the story of a middle-aged professor of literature, Moses Herzog, having a nervous breakdown because his wife Madeleine has left him after cheating on him with his best friend. It's also semi-autobiographical: Bellow's second marriage had ended five years earlier, and he then discovered his wife had been having an affair with his friend Jack Ludwig, a colleague at the University of Minnesota. As Louis Menand, the American critic and writer for the *New Yorker*, says, Bellow didn't have a nervous breakdown: he wrote *Herzog* instead.

The letters Herzog writes, in search of relief from his predicament, are random and open-ended; he's questioning everything. But he doesn't come to any sort of understanding in the way that Wilde does. Nothing makes sense. 'If I am out of my mind, it's all right with me,' he says in the opening line of the novel. For several months he's been obsessed with the need to 'explain, to have it out, to justify, to put in perspective, to clarify, to make amends' – all the things we're trying to do when we write those crazy, furious letters that we've no intention of sending. It had all started in the middle of a lecture: he had to break off and scribble down notes as they occurred to him. 'He was reasoning, arguing, he was suffering, he had thought of a brilliant alternative – he was wide-open, he was narrow; his eyes, his mouth made everything silently clear – longing, bigotry, bitter anger . . . Considering his entire life, he realised that he had mismanaged everything.'

Herzog is named after a minor character in James Joyce's *Ulysses*, so perhaps it's not surprising that his thought patterns are so unstructured and free-flowing, his letters so wide-ranging. 'He was writing letters to everyone out of the sun . . . He wrote endlessly, fanatically, to the newspapers, to people in public life, to friends and relatives and at last to the dead, his own obscure dead, and finally the famous dead' – including Schopenhauer, Nietzsche and Hegel.

To Dr Bhave, the Indian philosopher and follower of Gandhi:

> Dear Dr Bhave, I read of your work in the *Observer* and at the time thought I'd like to join your movement. I've always wanted very much to lead a moral, useful, and active life. I never knew where to begin. One can't become Utopian. It only makes it harder to discover where your duty really lies. Persuading the owners of large estates to give up some land to impoverished peasants, however . . .
>
> To Governor Stevenson: 'Just a word with you, friend . . .'

In an effort to deal with his break-up from Madeleine, and to decide what to do about his current girlfriend, Ramona, whom he loves but isn't sure about marrying, his mind leaps from an address to his academic colleague ('Dear Dr Mossbach, I am sorry you are not satisfied with my treatment of T. E. Hulme and his definition of Romanticism as "spilt religion" . . .') to hailing an old friend he hasn't seen for 15 years ('Dear Nachman, I know it was you I saw on 8th St. last Monday. Running away from me. It was you. My friend nearly 40 years ago – playmates on Napoleon Street. The Montreal slums. Nachman! Did you think I'd ask for the money you owe me? I wrote that off, long ago.') Which leads him into memories of his childhood, his family – and then, returning to Nachman, he realises he doesn't know where to send the letter – or any of the others he's drafting.

> Dear Mr President, Internal Revenue Regulations will turn us into a nation of book-keepers. The life of every citizen is becoming a business. This, it seems to me, is one of the worst interpretations of the meaning of human life history has ever seen. Man's life is not a business.

> Dear Dr Schrodinger, In *What is Life?* you say that in all of nature only man hesitates to cause pain . . .

Finally, after frenzied to trips to New York and Chicago, during which he gets himself into a car accident and is arrested while carrying a loaded gun, he returns to his beautiful but dilapidated summer house in rural Massachusetts. The house is full of insects and dead birds, and Herzog finds something oddly restful in the garden being too hopeless to do anything with: he's 'past regretting'. In search of peace and clarity he walks his land and begins a final week of letters:

Dear Sirs, The size and number of the rats in Panama City, when I passed through, truly astonished me. I saw one of them sunning himself beside a swimming pool. And another was looking at me from the wainscoting of a restaurant as I was eating fruit salad. Also, on an electric wire which slanted upward into a banana tree, I saw a whole rat-troupe go back and forth, harvesting. They ran the wire twenty times or more without a single collision. My suggestion is that you put birth-control chemicals in the baits. Poisons will never work (for Malthusian reasons; reduce the population somewhat and it only increases more vigorously).

Dear Herr Nietzsche – My dear sir, May I ask a question from the floor? . . . Nature (itself) and I are alone together, in the Berkshires, and this is my chance to understand. I am lying in a hammock, chin on breast, hands clasped, mind jammed with thoughts, agitated, yes, but also cheerful, and I know you value cheerfulness – true cheerfulness, not the seeming sanguinity of Epicureans, nor the strategic buoyancy of the heartbroken . . .

Every now and then he interrupts himself: 'Herzog! you must stop this quarrelsomeness and baiting of great men'. But it doesn't hold him up for long.

No, really, Herr Nietzsche, I have great admiration for you. Sympathy. You want to make us able to live with the void. Not lie ourselves into good-naturedness, trust,

> ordinary middling human considerations, but to question as has never been questioned before, relentlessly, with iron determination, into evil, through evil, past evil, accepting no abject comfort. The most absolute, the most piercing questions.

And finally Herzog writes to God:

> How my mind has struggled to make coherent sense. I have not been too good at it.

In the end, though, the letters seem to have worked their therapy. Talking to himself before Ramona arrives for dinner, he asks, 'But what do you want, Herzog?' and answers, 'But that's just it – not a solitary thing. I am pretty well satisfied to be, to be just as it is willed, and for as long as I may remain in occupancy.' He has nothing left to rant about: with 'the knowledge that he was done with these letters', he has reached a point of calm. He's no longer out of his mind – unless in the sense that the letters have taken him out of his mind and into a more peaceful place.

The advice you've always wanted to give

Malcolm Bradbury's *Unsent Letters*

The author of *The History Man* and *Eating People is Wrong* admitted to not usually being much of a letter writer. But he recognised the therapeutic uses of a letter, and developed his own technique to deal with the sackloads of unwanted mail he received from would-be writers (for which he blamed himself, having back in 1970 set up the original Creative Writing MA course at the University of East Anglia). His own 'unsent literary letters', drafted in reply and collected into a glorious *jeu d'esprit* of a book, say all the things he would have liked to say to his correspondents over the years if he'd had nothing better to do. Of course, as he's been writing these in his head anyway, resenting the intrusion into his own writing time and yet not able to ignore the thoughts, he hasn't really saved himself any time. But at least he's worked some of the exasperation out of his system.

This one is his ingenious response to the many would-be authors – in this case a woman who has, she tells him, written 35 remarkable but yet unpublished novels – who send him their manuscripts in search of advice on how to 'get started'. Whereas what they really want, explains Bradbury, is 'to get started on being published, which is a very different business from writing the books themselves'.

Dear Miss Bricktop,

Thank you so much for your letter and its massive enclosures. As you do so rightly assume, there is nothing we writers love more than giving our aid to the authors of the next generation who are all set to supersede us. And certainly I for one have always believed in doing everything I can on behalf of the up-and-coming young – or as it seems in your case, unless you write inordinately quickly, here-and-going middle-aged – writer. Believe me, I should not wish to do anything to add to your sense of rejection, which I can see must by now be considerable – though be reassured, a masochistic and paranoid temperament is a well-known sign of a great writer. If then I feel compelled to return these bulky and prodigious manuscripts to you at once, without actually reading them, you will understand it is for the very best of reasons.

The fact is, dear Miss Bricktop, you just happen to catch me at the most unfortunate of moments. Just the other day I strained my back, carrying about some royalty statements. My doctor, who is visiting me regularly, advises that on no account should I lift manuscripts of very great weight – especially any that begin 'In the beginning was the Word', as I see all of yours do. My oculist, who has just gone, has warned me that if I spend long hours over crabbed and ill-formed handwriting I shall not be word-processing for very much longer. And, even worse, the Tax Inspector has just been with the warning that I am now faced with a very stark choice. I can choose to spend all my time reading unpublished novels by other people, in which case he will provide me with comfortable circumstances to complete the task, such as a cell in Parkhurst; or else I must get some writing done at once and clear off my contribution to the National Debt, since the Chancellor has until only next April to balance his budget. I am sure you will agree that the only thing for me to do in the circumstances is to switch from reading to writing mode at once.

Or perhaps you will not; re-reading your letter I can see I could well be wrong. So please understand that there are yet more important reasons why I return your packet unperused. To be utterly frank with you, I am a terrible literary magpie. I should hate this information to get out, and I tell it to you in total confidence, but no sooner do I read the brilliant words written by some other author than I feel a vile temptation to appropriate them for my very own. This has become a profound dilemma for me, and I have discussed it with my priest, who serves fine counsel and an excellent Chablis. He, I fear, recommends that for a period, until my moral equilibrium is restored, I try to avoid reading anything not yet published by anyone else whatsoever. I know plagiarism is very fashionable indeed these days, but I am ethically opposed to it, except in the case of James Joyce's *Ulysses*. Thus I am trying my very best to do you a favour and ensure that when your books are published, as one day, if you keep up this kind of correspondence, they might be, they get an absolutely fresh, fair hearing, and are not confused with my own.

So, dear Miss Bricktop, I say again that I have decided with all regret to avoid reading your actual manuscripts, but of course this does not preclude me from offering you some sage literary advice. And I do have a few general thoughts on what makes a good and publishable writer that I tend to offer on all possible occasions. Briefly, a good and successful writer is to be distinguished by several qualities I would recommend you cultivate. A good writer, in my experience, is a good re-writer, who does not write a very large number of books but works back over the first one and gets it more or less right. A good writer is also someone who possesses a good typewriter, and knows how to use it; some of the most successful are effective with the Tippex as well. A good writer is usually a good reader, especially of the works of contemporaries (there are certain special exceptions to this, such as those who for medical, tax or ethical reasons must refrain from reading for a while, but this is generally true). A good writer is someone with a mind so fine that no idea can violate it, someone on whom no impression is lost, and someone who also has a relative, friend, or lover who happens to work in the editorial department of one of our leading publishing houses. And, above all, if I may say so, a good writer is almost never called P. S. Bricktop. May I recommend a pseudonym – something like John Le Carré, though not too much like it, to avoid confusion – and I think you may well find your chances are quite considerably improved.

But if all this fails, may I make a broader observation. I believe that in the literary life of this country we face a very severe social problem which is almost beyond our wits to solve. It is akin to the problem we have faced in industry, where there were far too many producers and not enough consumers. In Britain today, as is evident from my own postbag, everyone is writing, in your own case in quite inordinate quantity. On the other hand, perhaps because of this intensive creative industry, the number of readers appears to be dropping very dramatically. Is it not time, in a period when everyone has to think about alternative employment, to think of taking some of these writers, and re-training them as readers? This is a situation in which we are all responsible, and I rather wonder if you might feel inclined to take a pioneering role, Miss Bricktop? No, looking at your letter again, Miss Bricktop, I rather doubt it will find favour; please forgive the suggestion, brought on only by the arrival of a new postbag containing several rather bulky packages. No, I have a better idea. Why not pack up your parcel yet again, as you undoubtedly will, and send it to G. K. Chesterton? I know he loves to hear from people.

Yours sincerely,

Markemstein Braddlebonny

That brilliant blend of sympathy and self-deprecation is a polite disguise for the devastating put-down. And what about the Chesterton comment in the final lines? The writer and critic, who died in 1936, was well known for enjoying literary debate. But if it's true that, in response to an inquiry *The Times* once sent out to famous authors asking, 'What's wrong with the world today?', he responded simply, 'Dear Sir, I am. Yours, G.K. Chesterton,' then his answer to Miss Bricktop might have been far briefer than Bradbury's. If he were around to say anything more, it might be that 'What we call the new ideas are generally broken fragments of the old ideas,' as he concluded in his essay *On Reading*. 'You can find all the new ideas in the old books; only there you will find them balanced, kept in their place.' In other words, as Bradbury says, it's time people read more, and wrote less.

'I feel as if I'm going mad'

Olaf Olafsson's *Walking Into the Night*

The therapy doesn't always work. If what you're 'writing out' is more about guilt and remorse than anger or resentment, you may find that by re-living it you're only prolonging the pain. In the Icelandic writer Olaf Olafsson's 2003 novel *Walking Into the Night*, Christian Benediktsson writes endless letters to the wife he abandoned 20 years earlier, torturing himself with images of Elisabet and their children, without knowing where they are or whether he will ever post the letters.

Living in a Californian mansion as butler to the real-life media magnate William Randolph Hearst (the model for Charles Foster Kane in Orson Welles's *Citizen Kane*), Christian can maintain anonymity as a faceless staff member, anaesthetised by the daily routine of his work, and distracted by the challenge of keeping the rich and famous of 1930s American society sober while they are house-guests of his teetotal employer.

But at night, off duty, it's harder to keep the past at bay. Dreams and memories, not always distinguishable one from another, overwhelm him: how he left Elisabet for an actress he met on a business trip to New York; how his lover died after having an abortion; how he has never forgiven himself in relation to either of them. He pours his deepest thoughts into the letters, but this isn't the kind of therapy that clears the mind by letting it all out. It's an ongoing process, like writing a diary: it will remain unfinished business because he can't absolve himself. He can't stop writing, even if Elisabet will never read his letters.

This is how I see you in my mind's eye –

You're sitting at the piano in the living room, it's sunny outside. Einar comes in, you look up to greet him. How old would he be now, I ask myself from habit. Twenty-eight, if I'm not mistaken. Twenty-eight years old, imagine! The years run together in a single thread and I forget what came first and what happened later. He looks like me – yes, in fact I see myself as a young man as he puts down his briefcase in the hall and takes off his light-coloured coat. Why should he be carrying a briefcase? I can't explain it. But I'm always relieved by the sight of it.

You, on the other hand, have not changed. You're always the same. It's strange when I see Einar go over to you: you as you were when we first met, he a full-grown man. In earlier versions you are playing Mozart on the piano, but now I've managed to break free of him. I succeeded in the end. It wasn't easy. Now I see your fingers gently stroking the keys (I remember it always seemed as if you hardly needed to touch them), but all I can hear is the sound of a bird singing in the garden. '*Tschik, tschik.*' A wagtail, I guess.

I expect the twins are upstairs. There's no way I can conjure up a picture of them and I no longer look at the photo in the drawer as often as I used to. It confuses me. Puts time out of joint.

Maria is wearing a red summer dress. I see her cheek, faintly, as if in a mirror. She is fair, with shoulder-length hair. Delicately built like you, but taller. She is on her way downstairs when Einar comes in. The light streams towards her when he opens the door. She vanishes in the brightness and I lose sight of her.

That's how I picture you for myself. Sometimes while I'm awake. Sometimes in a dream.

Always the same.

Later . . .

You haven't changed. Einar is coming in; I know it's him, though I have difficulty picturing him in my mind. When I try, I invariably see myself as a young man.

The picture vanishes. Darkness falls on it, subjugating my mind and depriving me of sight. You are no longer in the living room, there is no one in the living room and no one opens the front door and says: 'Hello, it's only me! I'm home!' No one comes down the stairs in a red dress and vanishes in the brightness that floods in through the door. No one, nothing. There is nothing before my eyes but darkness.

Yet I can hear whispering. You're on the street in Reykjavik, people are watching you and putting their heads together. You know they're there but hurry away without looking at them, moving closer to the walls of the buildings with their concealing shadows. But the voices pursue you, you can't drive them away, even though you quicken your pace and begin to hum a tune.

'There she is . . . the wife of that man who vanished. I wonder where he went. Some people think he drowned himself. Or went abroad, taking all their money . . . Four children, imagine! The poor little mites . . .'

The whispering echoes in my head, accompanied by the tune you're singing to try to drown it out. It's as if someone keeps turning up the volume of a radio; I can't turn it down, and in the end I take to my heels to try to outrun it, clasping my hands over my ears.

I feel as if I'm going mad.

We no longer know if he's talking to Elisabet or to himself. At one point Christian says he is 'certain of finding comfort in all the letters I've been writing to you'. But they start to lose their therapeutic power, as he realises nothing he says will reconcile him to his past. 'The words I've been searching for. I know they won't do you any good, yet I still keep trying to find them.' He vacillates between hoarding the letters and throwing them away. Sometimes he even dreams of sending them. But where to? There's a strange incident in which Hearst's mistress, the actress Marion Davies, nearly dies after an overdose of pills, and Christian, finding her barely conscious with a note in her hand, throws the paper on the fire unread. As she wakes, Marion repeatedly tells Hearst not to read the note, and Christian reassures him that there was no note: whatever she had written remains her secret. Everyone writes things they don't, in the end, want others to read.

Then, when a forest fire threatens the mansion, Christian's picture ends up on the front page of the newspapers as the hero of the hour. His cover blown, he gets a letter from Elisabet's cousin in North Dakota, filling in the missing history with unbearable clarity. It tells him that she and the children had come to America in search of him (although he doesn't know that she tracked him to the Waldorf Astoria in New York, where he had stayed with his mistress – the same hotel built by John Jacob Astor whose last letter remained forever unsent when the *Titanic* went down). That Elisabet eventually gave up the search and went back to Iceland with Maria, who is now expecting her first child, and that Elisabet herself died nearly five years ago. But that Einar, who now has two children of his own, still lives with him in North Dakota. Einar, who in Christian's dreams looks like his own younger self, has been in America all this time.

The novel ends with Christian anticipating Einar's arrival at San Simeon and realising that he can't face him. The letters may have given him temporary relief, but they haven't exorcised the guilt, and he walks out into the night again.

> If anyone made enquiries after him, he asked the Chief to see that they were given a shoebox he had left behind containing a few small odds and ends, tied up with string.
>
> At the last moment, he had decided to leave the letters behind. He had contemplated them for a long time before taking them out of his bag and wrapping them in a handkerchief. He left the shoebox on his desk, the note to the Chief on top of the shoebox, the letters next to it.

'The shoebox and the letters are for my son,' he tells Hearst. So the letters will reach a sort of destination – the son rather than his mother. But nobody will know where to send a reply.

'I don't think you have the guts to shoot a rabbit'

Ernest Hemingway to Joseph McCarthy

Hemingway wrote so many letters that nearly 60 years after his death in 1961 they are still being collated (four volumes so far, taking us up to 1931: another 30 years still to go). And according to the editor of his *Selected Letters*, Carlos Baker, he used writing them as a form of therapy, the rough equivalent of the psychiatrist's couch, leaving many of them unsent. 'I might as well write it out now and maybe get rid of it that way,' he apparently told Pauline Pfeiffer, the second of his four wives, in 1926.

A lot of them are frankly hard to follow – the arguments often drunkenly chaotic and the spelling erratic: he can't be bothered to correct his mistakes, and when he does he gets even more worked up at having to pause in the headlong attack. (He also hoarded notes and communications from other people, including a telegram from Ingrid Bergman, who had starred in the 1943 film version of *For Whom the Bell Tolls*, congratulating him for winning the Nobel Prize for Literature in 1954. 'THE SWEDES ARENT SO DUMB AFTER ALL,' she wrote.)

By May 1950 he'd been living in Cuba for ten years, on a farm outside Havana that he'd bought with his third wife, Martha Gellhorn, and now shared with his fourth, Mary Welsh. He fished and wrote, working on *The Old Man and The Sea*, which would be published in 1951, and drank. His novel *Across the River and Into the Trees*, which was being serialised in *Cosmopolitan* magazine prior to publication, was getting a poor reception from the critics, and he was suffering leg pain from a 1918 shrapnel injury, so he probably wasn't in the best of moods.

Hemingway wasn't yet on Joseph McCarthy's list of 'unAmerican authors', or at least not publicly, because that wasn't released for another few years, but he'd already shown enough interest in left-wing politics (including writing essays for the Marxist *New Masses* magazine during the 1930s) to earn a place there. And McCarthy, Republican Senator for Wisconsin, was already making headlines by accusing Truman's Democrat administration of harbouring more than 200 known Communists in the State Department. The Tydings committee's five-month investigation into this claim held hearings from February to July 1950, and would have been halfway through when Hemingway was provoked into writing this tirade to McCarthy. (The committee concluded that McCarthy's accusations were unfounded, and rebuked him for squandering legislative resources at a critical moment of the Cold War, which might explain Hemingway's comment about tax-payers.)

It wasn't just the anti-Communist campaign that riled Hemingway, though. McCarthy was said to have falsified his war record with exaggerated tales of heroism – which is presumably what Hemingway is getting at in the references to lost limbs, number of wounds and the invitation to engage in a fight with no witnesses. Hemingway, whose instinct had always led him towards danger rather than away from it – he'd been wounded as an ambulance driver in the First World War, reported from the midst of the action in the Spanish Civil War and from one of the landing ships on D-Day in June 1944 – wouldn't have been impressed by any hint of spinelessness, especially since his own eldest son, Jack, had been awarded the Croix de Guerre for bravery after being parachuted into France to help the Resistance.

To SENATOR JOSEPH MCCARTHY, La Finca Vigia, 8 May 1950

Honorable Senator Joe McCarthy:

My dear Senator:

Quite a number of people are beginning to get tired of you and you have possibilities of becomeing a complete stranger. If you lost limbs or your head in the action in the Pacific everyone naturally would sympathise with you. But many people are merely bored since they have seen good fighters who had it in their time. Some of us have even seen the deads and counted them and counted the numbers of McCarthys. There were quite a lot of you but you were not one and I have never had the opportunity to count the numbers of your wounds and get any sort of reading on the comparison with how your mouth, repeat moth, get it straight mouth, goes off.

I know you were in a fine force and you must have been wounded really badly but Senator you certainly bore the bejeesus out of some tax-payers and this is an invitation to get it all out of your system. You can come down here and fight for free, without any publicity, with an old character like me who is 50 years old and weighs 209 and thinks you are a shit, Senator, and would knock you on your ass the best day you ever lived. It might be healthy for you and it would certainly be instructive.

So you are always welcome, kid, and in case you have dog blood, which I suspect, don't resort to sopoeanas (mis-spelled) but come on down all expenses paid and if you are a small Marine you can fight any of my kids and get a reputation. I have them that weigh from 152 to 186. You can fight any one. But afterwards me.

Good luck with the good part of your investigation and, if we can take off the part of the uniform you take when you go outside, and fornicate yourself. You would have a nice fight without witnesses and then you could tell it to all.

Yours always

Ernest Hemingway

Actually I don't think you have the guts to fight a rabbit; much less a man. Am old but would certainly love to take you quick. Or to see the kids take you slow and careful.

Yours always, and with great respect for your office

Ernest Hemingway

[Typed and signed twice by EH but perhaps not sent.]

It's so intemperate and peevish from the start, you can't believe he ever intended to send this. And that PS, a final shout, like ringing the doorbell and running away – even more childish, and signed off with the unanswerable 'with great respect': a pinch and a punch to you, and no returns. He had to have the last word.

(Given the number of enemies he created during his ten years in office, McCarthy must have been the non-recipient of a lot of unsent ranting therapy letters. Truman definitely wrote one, after McCarthy accused the entire Truman administration of selling out to the Communists: 'You are not even fit to have a hand in the operation of the Government of the United States. I am very sure that the people of Wisconsin are extremely sorry that they are represented by a person who has as little sense of responsibility as you have.')

A coda to all this: Hemingway is the one you might have expected to drink himself to death, but it was McCarthy who died of acute hepatitis, in 1957, at only 48. Hemingway outlived him by another four years, succumbing to suicide rather than alcohol.

V

And All Because Of A Letter . . .

So many 'If only's. If only Romeo had received Friar Lawrence's letter telling him Juliet wasn't really dead. If only Tess Durbeyfield had checked for a carpet before she pushed her letter under Angel Clare's door. If only . . .

Letters have always provided a handy plot device. The epistolary novels of the 18th and early-19th centuries relied on them to convey the entire narrative by recounting events from multiple viewpoints, and the format has never completely gone out of fashion. Twenty-first-century novels written as letters include the first-person bleakness of Lionel Shriver's *We Need to Talk About Kevin* (in which the story is told through the letters of the teenage killer's mother, Eva), as well as several novels constructed around letters to famous people (to Omar Sharif in Rachel Wyatt's *Letters to Omar*, and to Morrissey of the Smiths in Willy Russell's *The Wrong Boy*). Even in a purely narrative novel, the arrival of a convenient item of mail can be a shortcut through the plotline, filling in an essential bit of backstory or getting the writer out of a sticky patch by sending the drama in a new direction.

Letters provide both structure and suspense. Rachel Joyce's *The Unlikely Pilgrimage of Harold Fry* begins with Harold receiving a letter from an old friend with the news that she is dying. He writes a reply, but instead of sending it he walks past the postbox, and keeps walking – from Devon all the way to North Berwick – to deliver it by hand. In *Swimming Lessons* by Claire Fuller, Gil finds letters to himself from his long-missing wife hidden inside books throughout the house, left there with no idea of when, or if, or in what order he'll discover them.

And letters that don't behave as they should, that go astray, reach the wrong recipient, are intercepted en route or become blackmail material: these have even more dramatic potential. In Patricia Highsmith's *Carol*, it's an unfinished love letter to Carol from Therese ('I feel I stand in a desert with my hands outstretched, and you are raining down upon me. I will comb you like music caught in the heads of all the trees in the forest . . .'), left absent-mindedly inside a copy of *The Oxford Book of English Verse*, that reveals their affair to Carol's husband – as a result of which he pursues enough evidence to divorce her and get custody of their daughter.

Which brings us back to the 'If only's. If only Therese hadn't left the letter inside that book. If only Friar Lawrence hadn't left it to Friar John to deliver his letter to Romeo, and Friar John hadn't then got himself locked inside a suspected plague house for the night so that the letter remained unsent, then Romeo would have known that Juliet would be waking up any minute and waiting for him – and we'd have been spared one more murder and a double suicide.

And while we're on Shakespeare, who made full use of the wayward letter wherever possible, there's Hamlet: sent off on a boat with Rosencrantz and Guildenstern – and a letter from his uncle, the King, which (as he discovers by getting suspicious and reading it) contains instructions for him to be beheaded as soon as he reaches England. Hamlet sensibly swaps the letter for one substituting his companions' names for his own, and heads back to Denmark to join his family in one final scene of mass murder. So that in the closing minutes of the play we get the announcement that 'Rosencrantz and Guildenstern are dead' – the line that four centuries later inspired a whole new play about chance and probability and the perils of playing postman. In Tom Stoppard's 1967 play, Rosencrantz and Guildenstern have become the main characters and Hamlet a bit part. We see them opening the letter and realising that they are delivering Hamlet – their childhood friend – to his death. 'Wheels have been set in motion, and they have their own pace, to which we are . . . condemned.' In the final scene, they read it again, and realise that fate, like the toss of a coin, has literally condemned them: they will die instead of him. And all because of a letter.

The letter under the carpet

Thomas Hardy's *Tess of the D'Urbervilles*

Thomas Hardy's novels are *all* about wheels being set in motion, the plots driven by an accumulation of bad decisions and malign forces. For his Wessex dairy maid, it begins long before the mishap of her letter: first when her father has his head turned by the idea of being descended from landed-gentry d'Urberville stock rather than Durbeyfield peasantry, and then when Angel Clare chooses one of the other girls to dance with instead of her, and again when her guardian angel leaves her alone in the moonlight with her very distant cousin Alec d'Urberville. It's vicar's son Angel she wants from the start, but it's moustache-twirling, cigar-smoking Alec who seduces her and leaves her pregnant with a child that only lives a few weeks.

And, this being Hardy, when she does finally get together with Angel it's just tempting fate that, before their wedding, she decides she has to tell him about Alec and the baby, to make a clean breast of it all so that she can marry him with a clear conscience.

> Declare the past to him by word of mouth she could not; but there was another way. She sat down and wrote on the four pages of a note-sheet a succinct narrative of those events of three or four years ago, put it into an

> envelope and directed it to Clare. Then . . . she crept upstairs without any shoes and slipped the note under his door.

It takes a few more days – wondering at his non-reaction – for her to discover her mistake:

> She stooped to the threshold of the doorway, where she had pushed in the note two or three days earlier in such excitement. The carpet reached close to the sill, and under the edge of the carpet she discerned the faint white margin of the envelope containing her letter, which he obviously had never seen, owing to her having in her haste thrust it beneath the carpet as well as beneath the door.
>
> With a feeling of faintness she withdrew the letter. There it was – sealed up, just as it had left her hands. The mountain had not yet been removed.

Poor Tess: how mundane – and how utterly believable. Just imagine having summoned up the courage to tell your deepest secret, to pour out your heart thinking you have removed a mountain of guilt – and then finding it still waiting to be confronted the next day.

Would the letter have made a difference to the course of things if Angel had read it? Probably not: when she does tell him the truth, after their wedding, his reaction is cold and judgmental, a hideous, hypocritical inability to see that her past is no more faulty than his. He can't forgive her for not living up to his ideal of her (you almost find yourself thinking what a shame there was no coercive-control legislation then). But at least she would have been spared the double anguish of having to confess *twice*. So the letter doesn't change the outcome, but it perhaps changes how we see Tess – her courage, her honesty, her determination to do the right thing, make herself worthy of Angel – and it crystallises her role as a tragic heroine for whom nothing is going to turn out well.

Empty promises and lethal threats

Oscar Wilde's *The Picture of Dorian Gray*

The tricksy, capricious nature of letters is perfect material for Oscar Wilde. In *The Importance of Being Earnest*, Cecily invents an entire self-penned cycle of love letters charting the course of an imaginary engagement. In *A Woman of No Importance*, Mrs Arbuthnot's illegitimate son writes a letter to his newly acknowledged father insisting that he marry her to redeem her honour – but she stops him from sending it because she doesn't *want* to marry him. And letters play a recurring role in Wilde's dark novella *The Picture of Dorian Gray*.

On two significant occasions, 18 years apart, Dorian writes letters that remain unsent. Both are written out of terror and self-preservation, but the first is too late to do any good (which is why he doesn't post it). The second is a more considered affair, and pre-emptive: he takes care to have it ready before it's needed.

Having become besotted with the actress Sybil Vane through her stage performances, he breaks off their engagement in horrified disappointment when her genuine love for him turns out to have undermined her ability to act convincingly. She no longer believes in the parts she plays, now that she loves him in real life, yet without her on-stage talent she is of no interest to him. 'I loved you . . . because you realised the dreams of great poets and gave shape and substance to the shadows of art,' he tells her. 'You have thrown it all away . . . You have spoiled the romance of my life . . . Without your art you are nothing.' But it's after this gratuitous cruelty to her that he notices the first subtle change in his portrait, a realisation that terrifies him into writing a letter of remorse, begging her to take him back. He knows he is in danger of losing his soul, and that Sibyl's love, innocent and uncynical, might have saved him.

> He did not know what to do, or what to think. Finally, he went over to the table, and wrote a passionate letter to the girl he had loved, imploring her forgiveness, and accusing himself of madness. He covered page after page with wild words of sorrow, and wilder words of pain. There is a luxury in self-reproach. When we blame ourselves we feel that no one else has a right to blame us. It is the confession, not the priest, that gives us absolution. When Dorian had finished the letter, he felt that he had been forgiven.

Like Tess Durbeyfield, he discovers the therapeutic value of writing it all out.

But unlike Tess, he doesn't get as far as trying to deliver the confession, because Sibyl is already dead, having killed herself in her dressing room, destroyed by his rejection. (In fact Lord Henry Wotton, whose friendship has been a corrupting influence from the first few pages of the book, has already written to tell him this, but Dorian hasn't opened the letter: 'I have not read it yet, Harry. I was afraid there might be something in it that I wouldn't like. You cut life to pieces with your epigrams.' He was instinctively right, but not because of any epigrams.) And when

Henry tells him, all he can feel, rather than genuine sadness, is the drama of the situation.

> 'If I had read all this in a book . . . I think I would have wept over it. Somehow, now that it has happened actually, and to me, it seems far too wonderful for tears. Here is the first passionate love-letter I have ever written in my life. Strange, that my first passionate love-letter should have been addressed to a dead girl. Can they feel, I wonder, those white silent people we call the dead? Sibyl? Can she feel, or know, or listen?'

By the end of his interview with Lord Henry, he's been persuaded that Sibyl had only ever existed as a work of fiction – as Desdemona, or Ophelia, or Juliet – and that Sibyl herself was 'less real' than the characters she had portrayed on stage. Thrilling to the melodrama, shaking off the tragedy he has caused like dust from his jacket, he can only feel, 'It has been a marvellous experience. That is all. I wonder if life has still in store for me anything as marvellous.' And it somehow makes perfect sense that he should have written his one great love-letter – never sent – to a phantom.

Then we get the blackmail letter. Eighteen years after Sibyl's death, Dorian commits a murder, quite deliberately this time. And with a body in need of disposal, he calls in a chemist, Alan Campbell, to 'destroy it so that not a vestige of it will be left'. Ahead of Campbell's arrival, Dorian writes and addresses a letter – we never see its text – this time in calm calculation. When Campbell refuses, appalled, to co-operate on the basis of whatever past acquaintance they have, Dorian plays his trump card.

> 'I am so sorry for you, Alan,' he murmured, 'but you leave me no alternative. I have a letter written already. Here it is. You see the address. If you don't help me, I must send it. If you don't help me, I will send it. You know what the result will be. But you are going to help me. It is impossible for you to refuse me now . . . Now it is for me to dictate terms.'

It's a hideous trap. I always wonder, reading that passage, how dark our secrets need to be before they are enough to blackmail us with? And how far would we go to keep them safe? We never find out who the letter is addressed to, and we have no idea what is says. Because of the period – and because this is Oscar Wilde – we can guess it's to do with Campbell's sexuality. When the novel was first printed, some reviewers attempted to link the story to the Cleveland Street scandal of 1889, which centred on a male brothel frequented by a clientele that included members of the British political elite.

Campbell doesn't even need to read the letter; it remains unopened and he does what Dorian wants. A few chapters later there's a casual reference to his suicide. The letter, whatever its contents, might as well have been sent, because the alternative turned out to be far worse.

Letters without letters

Mark Dunn's *Ella Minnow Pea*

This beguiling, unsettling, perfectly constructed story describes itself as a novel without letters. In fact it's also a novel *in* letters and *about* letters (say the title aloud, and you get L, M, N, O, P in a neat run). It's set on a fictional American island named after Nevin Nollop, author of the pangram 'The quick brown fox jumps over the lazy dog'. When tiles spelling out the sentence begin falling, one by one, from Nollop's statue, inhabitants are forbidden from using the letters concerned.

So as the story proceeds – conveyed through correspondence between various islanders – the book is completed in an ever-shrinking alphabet: literally in unsent letters, in fact. This seems to have a strange effect on time itself: at first the plot starts to move faster, as the supply of available letters (and therefore words) becomes depleted and communication more perfunctory; then it slows right down to a stumbling, stop-and-start pace, as the various scribes resort to complex alternative spellings, so that the reader has to decode each word like a five-year-old just starting school. And humanity reduces along with the letters, the authorities becoming ever more fanatical, the community fearful and suspicious, in this literal dictatorship – a situation that can only be resolved if a new, shorter pangram can be found to replace the 'quick brown fox'. People are forced to police their own words and their neighbours', and all mail posted is scanned to check for forbidden characters.

The following letter from the narrator's father (written using the full alphabet because it won't be seen by the censors) is unsent – but not unread. Amos (who earns a living making ceramic vessels) leaves it on the kitchen table before being deported by the authorities. He hasn't time to write everything he wants, but – as you will discover if you read the book – it ultimately says all that matters.

Gwenette, loving spouse,
Ella, my Ella,
A slip-up near a police goon. Now only minutes away: a tap on the portal, then a hasty trip to Pier Seven. Will I see you two prior to my leave? I'm sorry to hear the news concerning Tassie. Who is her lawyer? Are they even allowing her counsel? I might suggest someone. There isn't much time, though.

Will you see me go, or will you remain at the Correctional Centre with Tassie? I will neglect something, I'm sure. Without your help. What a help you have –

Enough!

I simply can't do it anymore. And why should I? Why be so careful now? Moments away from transportation to the dreaded 'Pier of Goodbyes'. What's the point? What is there left to lose?

Like a retarded robot I go into the pre-programmed mode, placing my brain on high-alert to avoid these Nollop-frowned-upon devil letters. The devils aren't in

Japan! The devils are here. Satan is alive and well, right here in all his z-q-j-d-k-f-b, jumpy-brown-fox-slothful-pooch-quick-and-the-dead-glory – right here upon this devil's island of hatred and anger and unconscionable, inconsolable loss.

Hide this letter. Hide it well, but let me say the things that I must say. Before it's too late. Let me say that I love you both dearly. Let me say that I am so very sorry for returning to strong drink, for turning my back on you when you needed me most. Now that I have a voice, there are hundreds of other things I want to say. But cannot. Look into my heart and know them all.

And find it in your own hearts to forgive me.

You don't have to see me off. I know you're worried about Tassie. Be there with her, for her. But if you do come, please do me a small favour – a large favour, really. I'm not able to transport my miniature moonshine jugs to the pier. I would like to take them with me, though. You know that where I'm going they will be as good as money. You'll find them in my studio – stored together – all ten dozen of them. Half that number should suffice. Put them in one of the little crates; they'll be easier to convey that way.

Would you mind doing this one last thing for me? Pack my box with five dozen liquor jugs?

Thank you.

Be well. Be safe.

Until we meet again.

Your loving husband and father,

Amos

'Are you out there still?'

Paul Wilson's *Mouse and the Cossacks*

In *Mouse and the Cossacks*, eleven-year-old Mouse's imagination is a whole world of letters, sent and unsent. Mouse communicates entirely through the written word: she has been silent for nearly half her life ('You can hear the things people say because the sound of your own voice doesn't get in the way,' she points out), and all her conversations have to be written. Ordering a coffee means thrusting a message across the counter like an incompetent bandit holding up a building society.

'Sometimes I try to imagine what happens to all the words that get formed in people's heads but don't get spoken,' she wonders. She sends text messages to random phone numbers – and gets replies that create streams of casual philosophy. In response to Mouse's question, 'How many things that people wish for in a life do you suppose come true?' someone sends back, 'Do you think that, one day, someone should write the history of wishing?' She leaves messages for her dead brother pinned to tree trunks. In a long, fantastical one-sided correspondence with another friend (to whom she claims that she has no address, so that he can't write back) she creates an imaginary life for herself and her mother, living in a succession of non-existent hotels peopled by bizarre, invented characters.

And then she finds a stack of letters written by William, whose house they are, in fact, renting, over the course of 50-odd years since 1947: all sent to – and returned from – an address in Austria.

Mouse and the Cossacks is a book about communication, and the lack of it. Mouse thinks it would be helpful if people displayed their current 'happiness score' so that you'd know how to act around them; William, diagnosed with a terminal illness, has been writing letters while he still has time to make stuff known. We all live among untold stories, things people want to say and things people don't want to hear. Mouse is silent partly because of something she saw as a small child and was told to keep quiet about.

William's letters, to the daughter he has never met, create an ongoing account of how, as a captain in the British Army, he fell in love with her mother, Anna, an interpreter for the Cossack Army at the end of the war. Mouse starts visiting William in his nursing home, convincing the staff that she knows him and befriending a nurse called Alice. Sitting in silence beside his bed, she reads the letters to herself.

> My dear girl,
>
> I wish you could have seen the spectacle. Two thousand officers, many of them in dress uniform, some wearing medals from the civil war, from the tsar, gathered together in the barracks square in the sunshine, ready to leave the camp to meet with the British field marshal that afternoon.
>
> Around the square, their families had gathered to see them off. Some of them, it is true, were cautious, upset. One or two were even crying through fear and uncertainty. Anna had been readying Vasilenko in his

dress uniform. He had brushed aside her puzzlement about why it was necessary for two thousand men to be bussed across the valley to meet with one field marshal rather than have Alexander come to meet them here. He told her that he trusted the British. He had reassured his field officers when he had made his telephone calls the previous evening. General Domanov had already set off for the conference from his HQ in Lienz. Vasilenko told Anna not to fret, that he would be back between six and eight that evening. He kissed her on the forehead before climbing into the Fiat for the ride to Oberdrauburg a dozen miles away. She came to tell me this. She seemed finally reassured. She embraced me, for the first time unconcerned about openly showing her affection for me. A line of 60 trucks, each one filled with officers, followed the Fiat out of the compound, taking the salute of old men, young boys, widows, mothers, all of them lining the roadside. In the square the departing trucks threw up a haze of dust that hung in the air for a long time after they were gone.

Only when the last truck was out of sight was I taken to one side and asked to report to the major at HQ. He told me that there was no conference at Oberdrauburg, or anywhere else. There was to be no British Foreign Legion, no Italian enclave. Out of sight of the camp, the convoy had been flanked by a contingent of British armoured cars and armed motorcycle outriders. The Cossack officers were being taken to the Soviet zonal frontier at Judenburg, to be handed over to the Red Army.

William has no idea whether Anna survived, or what happened to her daughter (she knew instinctively it was going to be a girl), but his letters tell the whole story, needing her to know the truth – that he had no knowledge of the handover, that he spent years afterwards trying to find Anna and her people. 'What happened to you? Are you out there still?' And the letters aren't just another neat way of telling the backstory – they resonate right into the present, because in the end, it's the letters that give Mouse back her voice.

> I turn the last page of the letter over and lay it down on the bed. William's hand is resting free beside it . . . Then something makes me glance round. Alice is standing behind me in the doorway. I don't know how long she has been there.
>
> 'You read very well,' she says.
>
> For a moment I think she can see inside my head. Then I realise she has been listening.
>
> Then I realise I must have been reading out loud.

The wrong letter

Ian McEwan's *Atonement*

This is the kind of mistake you wake up screaming about – and one that's even more likely now it's so easy to press the 'Send' button in error.

Ian McEwan regularly gives letters a key role in his plots. In his Booker-Prize-winning novel *Amsterdam*, the composer Clive Linley mentally drafts a furious letter to newspaper editor Vernon Halliday, but stops short of writing it, aware that 'a letter sent in fury merely put a weapon into the hands of your enemy. Poison, in preserved form, to be used against you long into the future.' But Clive is so desperate to vent his anger that he can't help writing a brief, spiky postcard telling Vernon that he deserves to lose his job. His mistake, however, is to wait another day before posting it, and to use a second-class stamp, so that by the time the postcard arrives Vernon has indeed been dismissed, and what was intended as a statement of criticism ('You deserve to be *sacked*') becomes a gloating endorsement of his fate ('You *deserve* to be sacked'), provoking an enraged reaction that drives the book to its dark conclusion.

And in McEwan's most acclaimed novel, *Atonement* – the one many commentators say *should* have won the Booker – Robbie's letter to Cecilia has all the ingredients for trouble. It's written after a sexually charged encounter with her (in the course of which he broke her family's 200-year-old Meissen vase, and she stripped down to her underwear to retrieve the pieces from the fountain where they had fallen), and is designed to take the embarrassed edge off their meeting again, in public, at dinner that evening. But it's hampered from the start by awareness of their social differences in 1930s England, as well as by his physical attraction to her. She's the daughter of the big house, he's the son of their cleaning lady. For him work will be a necessity; to her it's a dream of liberation. He wants to train as a doctor; she is restless and dissatisfied by academic study. This letter is impossibly hard to write, every phrase and nuance a potential mis-step. In the struggle to strike the right tone and steer clear of dangerous ground, even the punctuation becomes a hazard.

> He typed the date and salutation and plunged straight into a conventional apology for his 'clumsy and inconsiderate behaviour'. Then he paused. Was he going to make any show of feeling at all, and if so, at what level?
>
> 'If it's any excuse, I've noticed just lately that I'm rather light-headed in your presence. I mean, I've never gone barefoot into someone's house before. It must be the heat!'
>
> How thin it looked, this self-protective levity. He was like a man with advanced TB pretending to have a cold. He flicked the return lever twice and re-wrote: 'It's hardly an excuse, I know, but lately I seem to be awfully light-headed around you. What was I doing, walking barefoot into your house? And have I ever snapped off the rim of an antique vase before?' He rested his hands

on the keys while he confronted the urge to type her name again. 'Cee, I don't think I can blame the heat!' Now jokiness had made way for melodrama, or plaintiveness. The rhetorical questions had a clammy air; the exclamation mark was the first resort of those who shout to make themselves clearer. He forgave this punctuation only in his mother's letters where a row of five indicated a jolly good joke. He turned the drum and typed an 'x'. 'Cecilia, I don't think I can blame the heat.' Now the humour was removed, and an element of self-pity had crept in. The exclamation mark would have to be reinstated. Volume was obviously not its only business.

He tinkered with his draft for a further quarter of an hour, then threaded in new sheets and typed up a fair copy. The crucial lines now read: 'You'd be forgiven for thinking me mad – wandering into your house barefoot, or snapping your antique vase. The truth is, I feel rather light-headed and foolish in your presence, Cee, and I don't think I can blame the heat! Will you forgive me? Robbie.' Then, after a few moments' reverie, tilted back on his chair, during which time he thought about the page at which his *Anatomy* tended to fall open these days, he dropped forward and typed before he could stop himself, 'In my dreams I kiss your cunt, your sweet wet cunt. In my thoughts I make love to you all day long.'

There it was – ruined. The draft was ruined. He pulled the sheet clear of the typewriter, set it aside, and wrote his letter out in longhand, confident that the personal touch fitted the occasion.

So the gun is loaded. The original typed draft, with its impetuous ending, is lying on his desk next to the innocuous hand-written copy he intends to give Cecilia. We're specifically warned of the danger: before heading out to the dinner, he gets ready 'as though preparing for some hazardous journey'.

But by the time he realises that he has put the wrong letter in the envelope, he has already given it to her highly strung, over-imaginative younger sister Briony, whom he meets en route. The strange destiny of this letter, though, is not the catastrophe he, or the reader, expects. It's a different one altogether. Cecilia, when she reads it, understands perfectly and accepts it as a gift, his error a glorious moment of Freudian serendipity. It is Briony, opening it before she hands it over, who is derailed. And it's Briony, her romantic, Latinate fantasies of gothic princesses destroyed by a very Anglo-Saxon reality, who takes the plot, and Robbie's entire life, down an utterly different path.

The wrong recipient

Patrick Gale's *The Whole Day Through*

Like Robbie's letter in *Atonement*, the love letter in Patrick Gale's *The Whole Day Through* goes astray through a younger sibling's interference. Where Briony's involvement is malicious, however, the motives of Ben's brother are thoroughly, if disastrously, well-meaning.

Ben and Laura, who last saw each other as student lovers 20 years earlier, run into each other at a hospital in Winchester. She is newly single after the latest in a series of bruising relationships, and has come back from Paris to look after her elderly mother, whose independence has been abruptly ended by a couple of falls. He is a doctor, unsatisfactorily married (to Chloe, whom they both knew at Oxford) and responsible since his mother's death for the care of his gay younger brother, Bobby, who has a form of Down's Syndrome. The book is an astute study of love and loss, romantic mistakes and fatal indecision (and also, incidentally, makes a robust case for people with learning disabilities to be able to enjoy full, happy, confident relationships of their own).

Ben and Laura resume the affair he broke off all those years back, and he decides that, this time, he's not going to let her go. The letter he writes to tell her is cautious and circumspect, aware of all the obstacles involved, but convinced that, ultimately, love will be enough to see them through.

Darling. You always said – you probably don't remember – we should never call each other that because it's what people call lovers they no longer love. So I'm sorry but I like it. I like its sturdy Saxon feel. Would deorling be less offensive? (Don't be impressed – just looked that up on the net.)

Your wonderful little visit to find me at work, totally unlooked for, unearned, has sent my mood rocketing and sod work, blow patients, I want to share it with you. You know I'm hopeless on the phone and not much better at explaining myself face to face. There are already several versions of this torn up in the office bin and still I'm stumbling.

We couldn't talk when you visited but perhaps that was a good thing if it stopped me blurting things that should be said with care. But now that I've had a while to think everything seems so clear, so simple suddenly, as if you'd blown the clouds away and all the shades of grey were gone.

I love you and I want to be with you always, whatever it takes and whatever compromises or sacrifices that involves me in and mess that means wading through.

Bobby will cope. He'll adjust and cope, of course he will. It's taken this time of worry and not talking to make me see I had my priorities in a twist and I've been crazily over-protective of him. Change is a part of living and he has to get used to it if he's to have independence.

But all of this assumes agreement on your part. Typical male bloody arrogance, I can hear you say. My behaviour has offered you an insult that would perfectly entitle you to tell me to bog off. Oh but I hope you won't. Can you ever forgive me? Can we somehow not forget but draw a line, at least, and start again? Christ, I hope so.

I probably won't post this, my deorling. I think I'm too shy. Either that or I'm just rehearsing on paper, building up my courage for the things I need to tell you. I love you and all will be well. All my love. Absolutely all of it. Bx

Unfortunately, when he says 'All will be well,' he's reckoning without his brother's gift for misdirected good intentions. Given Ben's concern to take care over his words, and the fact that he has already torn up several earlier drafts and admits that he probably won't post this one, it's the ultimate irony that Bobby finds the 'nice letter', assumes it's for Chloe, and, buoyed up by the prospect of his own hot date with a train driver, thinks he's doing Ben a favour by posting it to her in London . . .

Where Robbie sent the wrong letter in *Atonement*, Ben's letter has been mailed to the wrong person, and, like Robbie, he can't call it back. And because – circumstantially – the whole letter can be read as applying to Chloe as much as to Laura, it's not a disclosure of infidelity, but rather an endorsement of his marriage. Instead of cutting himself loose from it, Ben has accidentally tightened its knots.

The withheld letter

Edith Wharton's *The Reef*

Edith Wharton novels so often turn on characters reaching a moral crossroads – a point from which unstoppable events are set in motion by the choice they make, even as you're begging them to step back, do the other thing. In *The Reef*, it all starts with a letter. Or rather, a telegram followed by several letters.

George Darrow is just leaving London, en route to visit Anna Leath, the woman he loves, at her house in France, when a telegram from her is thrust through the train window, putting him off for two weeks: 'Unexpected obstacle. Please don't come till thirtieth.'

Stubbornly refusing to turn back, and then meeting exuberant, engaging (today we'd probably call her 'bubbly') young Sophy Viner by chance at Dover, Darrow crosses to Calais with her, and as they reach Paris the letters permeate both the story and the descriptive detail of the narrative. 'I'm expecting a letter,' is one of the first things he says to Sophy. He spends the first quarter of the book waiting for Anna's explanation to arrive, and repeatedly being told 'Pas de lettres' by the hotel clerk in Paris. Angry with Anna and intrigued by his new friend, he persuades Sophy to write to her friends and delay her onward travel – but is then irritated by watching her faltering, immature, 'scratching' attempts at a letter. He can't help comparing them – almost sexually – to the firm strokes of Anna's writing, and the letter from her that might even now be waiting for him.

But there's still no word from Anna, so instead he takes Sophy to dinner, and to the theatre, after which she resurrects her plan to join her friends.

> 'I asked Mrs Farlow to telegraph as soon as she got my letter.'
>
> A twinge of compunction shot through Darrow. Her words recalled to him that on their return to the hotel after luncheon she had given him her letter to post, and that he had never thought of it again. No doubt it was still in the pocket of the coat he had taken off when he dressed for dinner. In his perturbation he pushed back his chair, and the movement made her look up at him.
>
> 'What's the matter?'
>
> 'Nothing. Only – you know, I don't fancy that letter can have caught this afternoon's post.'
>
> 'Not caught it? Why not?'
>
> 'Why, I'm afraid it will have been too late.' He bent his head to light another cigarette . . .
>
> 'Oh dear, I hadn't thought of that! But surely it will reach them in the morning?'
>
> 'Some time in the morning, I suppose. You know the French provincial post is never in a hurry. I don't believe your letter would have been delivered this evening in any case.' As this idea occurred to him he felt himself almost absolved.

There's a constant tension between the letter Darrow is waiting for, and the one he hasn't sent. Finding it in his pocket later that night, he initially intends to post it, but instead, from a mixture of disappointment, self-justification, and enjoyment at being able to indulge his companion, he convinces himself that Sophy *wants* to stay in Paris with him.

> After all, if she had been very anxious to join her friends she would have telegraphed them on reaching Paris, instead of writing. He wondered now that he had not been struck at the moment by so artless a device to gain more time. The fact of her having practised it did not make him think less well of her; it merely strengthened the impulse to use his opportunity. She was starving, poor child, for a little amusement, a little personal life – why not give her the chance of another day in Paris? If he did so, should he not be merely falling in with her own hopes?

But he isn't absolved, and the unsent letter won't go away – not just the long-term consequences (because their presence together in Paris is observed and comes back to haunt him when he eventually reaches Anna's house), but because Sophy keeps mentioning it.

'Do you happen to remember,' she asks him at the end of the next day, 'what time it was when you posted my letter?' He desperately doesn't want to tell her that he didn't post it at all, reasoning that 'most wrongdoing works, on the whole, less mischief than its useless confession,' and aware that in this case 'a passing folly might be turned, by avowal, into a serious offence'.

Which is exactly what happens. He keeps playing with the idea that it's what she wanted all along, but in the end he undermines all his own logic and finds himself declaring that he did it on purpose, to keep her in Paris with him, tripping himself up with his own conscience and in the process inflating the incident into an affair he had never intended.

And by the time his letter from Anna arrives, ten days later, the damage is done.

VI

Not-Quite Letters

Some letters never quite make it onto paper at all, but leave a letter-shaped hole where the words might have been.

History and literature are littered with events where the absence of an anticipated message makes all the difference. Think of Neville Chamberlain, at the start of September 1939, waiting for Hitler's answer to his ultimatum, and none coming. It was two days since Germany's invasion of Poland, and letters were being hand-delivered by diplomats in embassies around Europe threatening war unless German forces withdrew: British ambassador Sir Nevile Henderson to Foreign Minister von Ribbentrop's interpreter in Berlin, French ambassador Robert Coulondre to Ribbentrop himself (oh, and Unity Mitford handed in a suicide note, along with her signed portrait of the Führer, at the Bavarian Ministry of the Interior in Munich). But there was no response from Hitler.

At 11.15 a.m. on 3 September, Chamberlain had to tell his waiting nation: 'This morning the British Ambassador in Berlin handed the German Government a final note stating that, unless we heard from them by 11 o'clock that they were prepared at once to withdraw their troops from Poland, a state of war would exist between us. I have to tell you now that no such undertaking has been received, and that consequently this country is at war with Germany.'

I've always wondered how the hoped-for 'undertaking' might have arrived. As a letter? A telegram? Perhaps a long-distance phone call? But at any rate, it didn't come.

More recently, and less significantly (although it caused a political earthquake at the time), Boris Johnson fell into a letter-shaped hole of his own making in the aftermath of the June 2016 EU Referendum. David Cameron's surprise resignation on 24 June, the morning after the vote, meant there was suddenly a vacancy for a new prime minster, and Boris was confidently expected (by himself and a large chunk of the country) to fill it. But first he had to secure the support of his own party – key among whom was fellow Leave campaigner Andrea Leadsom, Minister of State for Energy in David Cameron's government. She was being touted as a possible leader herself, but was biding her time, sounding out the other candidates to see what Cabinet posts they might offer her. At some point on 29 June, phone calls from the Boris team (which included Michael Gove) confirmed that she would have one of three top jobs in a Boris cabinet – Deputy Prime Minister or Chancellor or Brexit negotiator. Boris agreed to confirm this in a letter that day and follow it up publicly with a tweet. From then on, everything went pear-shaped.

Tim Shipman's book on the Referendum and its outcome, *All-Out War*, describes how Boris got the letter written, and took it with him to the Tories' summer party at the Hurlingham Club in south-west London, where (leaving early to work on the speech that was due to launch his campaign the following morning) he gave the letter to another member of his team to pass on to Andrea Leadsom. But she wasn't there – and texts offering to get the letter to her wherever she was failed to produce a result. The promised tweet might have saved the deal, but in the general mix-up that wasn't sent either: a not-quite tweet piling in on top of the not-quite letter. Just after 9.30 that evening, Andrea Leadsom texted Boris to say that she was withdrawing her support and standing for the party leadership herself. Within 24 hours, the non-appearance of the letter had changed everything. Michael Gove, rattled by his friend's chaotic approach, also jumped ship and launched his own bid, the Boris campaign imploded – and Theresa May was handed the premiership on a plate.

The offer that never materialises, the subject so important that you can't articulate it, the imagined response to some future event – there's something particularly eloquent about all these not-quite letters: the words unsaid, their potential forever unfulfilled. In her 1963 memoir *Instead of a Letter*, Diana Athill recalls waiting two letter-less wartime years to hear from her fiancé (at the end of which she receives a 'formal note' asking her to release him from the engagement so that he can marry someone else): 'The times when the pain was nearest to the physical – to that of a finger crushed in a door, or a tooth under the drill – were not those in which I thought "He no longer loves me" but those in which I thought "He will not even write to tell me that he no longer loves me".'

For Agatha Christie, the letter not sent is equivalent to Sherlock Holmes's dog that didn't bark. In *The Moving Finger*, Miss Marple deduces the identity of the poison pen writer (also the murderer) from the *absence* of a particular anonymous letter in a village where all the other residents seem to have been targeted. 'It was really, you see, Mr Symmington's one weakness. He couldn't bring himself to write a foul letter to the woman he loved.'

And one happier example: Jane Austen turns the not-quite letter into an art, like a painter defining her subject by describing the background rather than the thing itself. What better way for Elizabeth Bennet to announce her engagement (and her impending installation as chatelaine of Pemberley) than by flirting around the edges of the news without ever actually mentioning it, and by teasing her aunt with the letter she *hasn't* written.

> I would have thanked you before, my dear aunt, as I ought to have done, for your long, kind, satisfactory detail of particulars; but to say the truth, I was too cross to write. You supposed more than really existed. But *now* suppose as much as you choose; give a loose to your fancy, indulge your imagination in every possible flight which the subject will afford, and unless you believe me actually married, you cannot greatly err. You must write again very soon, and praise him a great deal more than you did in your last. I thank you again and again, for not going to the Lakes. How could I be so silly as to wish it! Your idea of the ponies is delightful. We will go round the Park every day. I am the happiest creature in the world. Perhaps other people have said so before, but not one with such justice. I am happier even than Jane; she only smiles, I laugh.

Only in the last two lines does she finally crack and mention specifics:

> Mr Darcy sends you all the love in the world, that he can spare from me. You are all to come to Pemberley at Christmas. Yours, &c.

There is, incidentally, a strong argument at the end of *Pride and Prejudice* for *not* preserving on paper the emotions, possibly transient, of a particular hour. An earlier letter, the one in which Darcy justifies his actions in relation to Mr Wickham and Mr Bingley respectively, has evidently been kept by Elizabeth – because after their engagement she offers to burn it. Its significance for both of them is immense. It's by reading and re-reading it at the time that Elizabeth realises how badly she has misjudged many of the book's events so far. As for Darcy, he is torn between hoping it helped to change her opinion of him – and hoping she has destroyed it. 'There was one part especially . . . which I should dread your having the power of reading again.'

Her response is unequivocal. 'Think no more of the letter,' she tells him. 'The feelings of the person who wrote and the person who received it are now so widely different from what they were then that every unpleasant circumstance attending it ought to be forgotten.' In other words, it was one of Janet Malcolm's 'fossils of feeling'.

Twelve letters *not* written by Rupert Brooke

In 1912 the English poet, his romantic life already complicated by affairs with both men and women, fell in love with the Irish actress Cathleen Nesbitt after seeing her play Perdita in *A Winter's Tale*. (Cathleen was later to develop a nice line in playing grandmothers to a certain class of matinee idol – she was Cary Grant's in *An Affair to Remember*, and Simon Williams's in *Upstairs Downstairs* – but in the early decades of the 20th century she was leading lady in countless productions on Broadway and the London stage.) Over the next three years Brooke bombarded her with marriage proposals and wrote her more than 80 letters (the last of them just a few weeks before he died in 1915, from blood poisoning, on his way to Gallipoli). This one is more about what he doesn't say than what he does, as words themselves seem to become inadequate.

> From Chateau Lake Louise, Laggan, Alta. Canada,
> 2 September 1913
>
> Liebes Kind (that's German for dear child),
>
> . . . I've nothing to tell you, except that the mountains are . . . and the lake is . . . and the snow and the trees are . . . but it would take me weeks to get out what they are, and I haven't time, for I want this letter to go today or tomorrow. Suffice it that they are wonderful.

Then, after describing an encounter between an Irish land agent and the native Indians on a reservation he had visited, he changes tack in exasperation and ends:

> This is a stupid letter. What I want to do is write you letters as follows
>
> (1) on Good
> (2) "
> (3) "
> (4) on Truth
> (5) on Love
> (6) "
> (7) on Dramatic Art
> (8) why all modern actors and actresses are so bloody bad.
> (9) why you may be some good, if you're carefully educated
> (10) what you're like -
> (11) what I'm like.

(12) what Life's like.

There's 12 letters. I wonder if I shall ever write them.

Anyway, from Vancouver (which I'm nearing) I'll write again, better.

For the present, my lovely child, Good be with you,

Your
Rupert

Perhaps Brooke dreamed up so many letters it didn't matter if some of them weren't quite written – or read. A few weeks later, on 12 October, writing again to Cathleen from the SS *Sierra* somewhere in the Pacific, he tells her of another one she may, or may not, receive.

My very dear,

I scribbled a few lines to you just before I started. But I gave the letter to a frightful rough-neck who was hanging about the wharf – we were just off – so he may have pouched the stamp and destroyed the letter.

Ozard of wiz for tea

Jennings and Darbishire write postcards home

Sometimes, fulfilling the *requirement* to compose a letter tips the writer over the edge. Generations of children, challenged with the task of multiple thank-you letters after Christmases and birthdays, would probably agree. And Anthony Buckeridge's mid-20th-century school stories, in which unpredictable events are regularly set in train by the strange logic of the 11-year-old brain, provide a rich seam of exchanges – written and otherwise – that don't quite conform to standard rules of correspondence. In the first of the series, arriving for their first term at Linbury Court Preparatory School in *Jennings Goes to School* (1953), Jennings and fellow new boy Darbishire are supplied with postcards and pens and instructed to write home.

> 'Who do I have to write to, sir?' asked Darbishire.
>
> 'Not "who", "whom"', corrected Mr Wilkins. 'To your mother and father, of course . . . No point in writing to the Archbishop of Canterbury; he won't be interested. Tell them you've arrived safely.'
>
> 'But they know that, sir,' said Darbishire. 'My father came down with me.'
>
> 'Can't help that,' said Mr Wilkins. 'School rules say,

"Write postcard home." All right then, write postcard home. Won't do any harm, will it?'

Darbishire decided to assure his parents that he was concerned about the state of their health. He headed his card, 'Linbury Court Preparatory School, Dunhambury, Sussex,' in huge, sprawling writing that covered more than half the postcard. 'My dearest Mother and Father,' he went on in letters half an inch high and nearly twice as broad, and discovered that there was only enough space left for one more line. 'I hope you are quite – ' He stopped, having completely filled up the available space. There was just room for a full stop, so he put that in and took his effort up for Mr Wilkins' approval.

Mr Wilkins adjusted his eyes to the outsize script and blinked.

'I hope you are quite – ?' he read out, bewildered. 'I hope you are quite, what?'

'No, not quite what, sir,' corrected Darbishire gently. 'Quite well.'

'So one might gather,' expostulated Mr Wilkins. 'But you haven't said that. You can't say "I hope you are quite, full stop." It's nonsense!'

'I hadn't got room for any more, sir,' explained Darbishire. 'And it's all right, really, 'cos my father'll know by the full stop at the end that I'd finished and wasn't called away unexpectedly in the middle or anything, sir.'

'But don't you see, you silly little boy, it doesn't make sense? How's your father going to know what it is "quite" that you hope he is? For all he knows, you might be going to say you hope he's quite – '; Mr Wilkins was unable to think of a suitable comparison.

'But it's bound to mean quite "well", sir,' reasoned Darbishire. 'After all, you guessed it, and if you can, sir, I'm sure my father could, and I wouldn't be likely to mean I hope you're quite "ill", would I, sir?'

Mr Wilkins, unconvinced, gives Darbishire a new postcard and tells him to start again.

Jennings' first attempt confuses Mr Wilkins even further (although it may help readers to know that the boys call Mr Carter 'Benedick' because he pronounces '*benedicto, benedicata*' after meals; that Jennings' new classmates include a boy called Atkinson and another called Temple – known as Bod for reasons too long to explain here; and that 'ozard' is the opposite of 'wizard'):

What should he say? His mother had told him to be sure to pay his pound into the school bank as soon as he arrived. He could say he had done that, for a start. He was richer than Darbishire because he had only got a pound less fourpence halfpenny. What else? Well, there was that frightfully funny joke Mr Carter had made about his having bubonic plague. What was it they called Mr Carter? Benny something? And it had something to do with the grace that Bod could translate, because he was a brain at Latin. Oh, yes, and that shepherd's pie for tea had been lovely. Surely he had enough material now . . .

Dear Mother,

I gave mine in to Mr cater Darbsher has spend 4½ of his my healthser ticket was in my pocket he said I had got

> bubnick plag it was a jok he is called Benny Dick toe I think it is. We had ozard of wiz for tea Atkion says wiz is good and oz is garstly so do I.
>
> Love John.
>
> PS Temple is a brain, he is short for dogs boody.

This one, too, remains unsent, for obvious reasons, as do another five drafts.

> The dormitory bell was ringing an hour later when Mr Wilkins reluctantly accepted Jennings' postcard. It was his seventh attempt and Mr Wilkins knew what it meant because Jennings, with infinite patience, had explained it. But to Mr and Mrs Jennings, who had no interpreter to help them, the postcard's message remained for ever a mystery.

A case, then, of a letter that *was* sent, but might as well not have been.

The kind of words that burn the paper they are written on

Lord Peter Wimsey to Harriet Vane

Dorothy L. Sayers's fictional detective Lord Peter Wimsey takes five years – and three books – to win the heart of novelist Harriet Vane, the woman he has saved from the gallows (and thereby put under impossible obligation to him). In *Gaudy Night*, the 1935 Oxford-based novel where she finally agrees to marry him, they do a lot of anguished not-writing to each other.

At one point there's an unseen, unread note written by Harriet to Peter on her way to a potentially dangerous encounter, scribbled in pencil and put away in her bag because 'if she got killed . . . perhaps it would be only decent to apologise beforehand'. (Whether she was apologising for her stupidity in letting it happen – or for causing grief to someone she cares about more than she has up to now acknowledged – is open to debate.) Later that night, the danger past, she destroys it without re-reading it. 'Even the thought of it made her blush,' says Sayers. 'Heroics that don't come off are the very essence of burlesque.'

In another chapter, challenged with writing to him about an incident she knows will hurt his pride, she takes five attempts to draft the letter – variously rejecting them as stiff, ineffectual, disapproving or fulsome – before managing a version she is happy with. 'Would anybody believe it could take . . . two hours to write a simple letter?' she asks herself. But Harriet's hesitation comes from hyper-awareness of her situation: she knows full well what a hazard a letter is, and is 'sensitive to the lightest breath of innuendo in her own words'. (And she sends it in the end. 'She put the letter resolutely into an envelope, and addressed and stamped it,' says Sayers. 'Nobody, having put on a twopenny-halfpenny stamp, was ever known to open the envelope again,' she adds, with more certainty than many of the letter-writers in this book.)

Peter, meanwhile, treats his own feelings with a gloomy self-mockery that keeps their true seriousness at a safe distance from both of them, while cheerfully threatening to propose to her on certain regular dates, including his birthday, and Guy Fawkes Day – and April Fool's Day. Yet there is enough emotional charge between them for her to notice when the expected letter *doesn't* arrive by the first post on 1 April. When it does appear (the fourth delivery of the day – a luxury hard to imagine now), Harriet tosses it aside, telling the friend she happens to be with, 'It's nothing. I know what's in it.' But it isn't nothing. The proposal, and the banter it's wrapped in, may be glib and offhand, but buried in the middle of the letter is a totally serious comment about the danger of putting feelings into words.

Dear Harriet

I send in my demand notes with the brutal regularity of the income-tax commissioners; and probably you say when you see the envelopes 'Oh, God! I know what this is.' The only difference is that, some time or other, one *has* to take notice of the income-tax.

Will you marry me? – It's beginning to look like one of

> those lines in a farce – merely boring till it's said often enough; and after that, you get a bigger laugh every time it comes.
>
> I should like to write you the kind of words that burn the paper they are written on – but words like that have a way of being not only unforgettable but unforgivable. You will burn the paper in any case; and I would rather there should be nothing in it that you cannot forget if you want to.
>
> Well, that's over. Don't worry about it.

He then continues:

> My nephew . . . is cheering my exile by dark hints that you are involved in some disagreeable and dangerous job of work at Oxford about which he is in honour bound to say nothing. But I know that, if you have put anything in hand, disagreeableness and danger will not turn you back, and God forbid they should. Whatever it is, you have my best wishes for it . . .
>
> Yours, more than my own,
>
> Peter Wimsey.

And that final paragraph has more impact than any number of eloquently worded proposals, because Harriet reads it as an admission of equality that she had not expected, something that 'not one man in ten thousand would say to the woman he loved, or to any woman'. It's a turning point for both of them, and the beginning of a new understanding: she starts to see the possibility of marriage to him in a new light, and her response (although in many ways another 'non-letter', because she can't talk about the mystery she's investigating at her former college) gives him a rare glimpse of hope by its total lack of resentment or petulance. 'I wish I could tell you; I should be very glad of your help . . . Thank you for not telling me to run away and play – that's the best compliment you ever paid me.'

(Interestingly, the start of the subsequent book, *Busman's Honeymoon*, takes the form of a classic epistolary novel. Written entirely in letters between the couple's friends, discussing their engagement and describing their wedding from every angle, the opening chapters convey the unmistakable sense of a genuine love match – and make up for every letter Peter and Harriet *didn't* manage to write to each other.)

'Darling Fascist Bullyboy, give me some more money'

The Young Ones to the bank manager

In the 'Cash' episode of the cult eighties BBC comedy *The Young Ones* the student housemates are so skint during a pitilessly hard winter that Neil the hippy is reduced to serving up plates of snow and announcing it as 'risotto', and, to keep the fire going, Vyvyan has, with great magnanimity, 'personally burnt everything Neil owns'. Then Neil has an idea . . .

Neil: [holding a letter] Guys, guys, guys. Guys, I think I've solved our money problem. I'm writing to my bank manager. See what you think, OK: 'Dear Bank Manager.'
Mike: Yeah?
Neil: Well, that's it. I'm quite pleased with it so far, though.
Mike: Oh, well, it's a strong opening, certainly.
Vyvyan: I don't like the 'Dear'. Sounds a bit too much like 'Will you go to bed with me?'
Mike: Well spoken, Vyvyan. Uh, what do you think instead?
Vyvyan: Uh, what about . . . 'Darling'?
[everyone concurs]
Neil: [writing] 'Darling Bank Manager . . .'

Rick: No, no, no, no, *no*, not 'Bank Manager', it's far too crawly bum-lick. Tell it like it is, put 'Fascist Bullyboy'!

Neil: 'Darling Fascist Bullyboy.'

Mike: That's nice, yes, so far so good. So what do you want to say?

Neil: Well, basically, I want to ask him if I can have, like, an extension on my overdraft, but I know there must be a better way of putting it than that.

Mike: Well, what about, 'Give me some more money'?

Vyvyan: 'You bastard!'

Neil: Don't you think that's a bit strong?

Mike: Ah, Neil, people like that respect strength.

Neil: Yeah, you're right. Uh, 'Darling Fascist Bullyboy, give me some more money, you bastard.' Uh . . . 'Love, Neil.'

Vyvyan: Not 'Love, Neil'! That sounds far too much like 'Come and get it like a bitch-funky sex machine!'

Neil: Yeah, you're right. Uh . . . uh, what about 'Yours sincerely'?

Rick: Oh, come off it, Neil. If you're going to be that sycophantic, why don't you go round there now and stick your tongue straight down the back of his trousers?

Neil: Oh, no, no, I know, I know, why not put 'Boom shanka'? It means, 'May the seed of your loin be fruitful in the belly of your woman.'

Rick: And what makes you think your bank manager's a man?

Neil: His beard.

Mike: He'll never understand 'Boom shanka'. You'll have to write the whole thing out.

Neil: Right, OK, here we go. 'Darling Fascist Bullyboy, Give me some more money, you bastard. May the seed of your loin be fruitful in the belly of your woman, Neil.'

Rick: Well, if that doesn't work, I don't know what will.

But then Mike notices that the fire is running low, and the most memorable begging letter Neil's bank manager will never receive goes up in flames.

Mrs Wilcox's scribbled note

and other retracted letters in E. M. Forster's *Howards End*

Howards End, the novel that famously stressed the importance of understanding connections (between ideas and events as well as between people), is full of letters sent and regretted, promised and unsent, letters that are expected, or talked of, or that might be written at some future date…

It's the meeting of two families. The Schlegels represent Art and Ideas, the Wilcoxes the world of Business – and everything that happens in the book is a result of the clash between these two cultures. The novel opens with a series of letters from Helen Schlegel to her sister Margaret (written from Howards End, the Wilcoxes' country house, where she is a guest), each signed off with a cryptic 'Burn this', and concluding with the news that she has agreed to marry Paul Wilcox: 'Dearest dearest Meg, I do not know what you will say: Paul and I are in love – the younger son who only came here Wednesday.'

Within a day of which, she sends a telegram to say, 'All over. Wish I had never written. Tell no one: – Helen.'

For 34 chapters, until people start talking openly to each other, everything significant is consigned to letters, many of which we never get to read. When, a few years after Mrs Wilcox's death, the widowed Henry Wilcox asks Margaret to marry him – in a proposal which Forster says was 'not to rank among the world's great love scenes' – she repeatedly tries to shut him up by telling him she will write to him. She keeps the interview 'in tints of the quietest gray', explains Forster, and in the end, in response to her 'You will have a letter from me', he can only say in bewilderment, 'I wish I had written instead. Ought I to have written?'

She does accept his proposal, but that is only the start of her difficulties in communicating with him: they speak different languages (his the world of commerce and contracts, hers of culture and ideas) and they frequently fail to understand each other. Later, trying to deal with the discovery – in the most public of circumstances, at his daughter's wedding – that he had kept a mistress ten years earlier while married to his first wife, she writes to him,

> My dearest boy, this is not to part us. It is everything or nothing, and I mean it to be nothing. It happened long before we ever met, and even if it had happened since, I should be writing the same, I hope. I do understand.

Then she crosses out the last line because, she reasons, 'Henry could not bear to be understood'. Then she crosses out 'it is everything or nothing', because 'Henry would resent so strong a grasp of the situation'. Finally, she tears it up completely and writes a letter to her sister instead.

At the heart of the book, though, is the note written by the first Mrs Wilcox on her deathbed, bequeathing her house to Margaret rather than to her own family.

> To my husband: I should like Miss Schlegel (Margaret) to have Howards End.

It's unsigned, undated and forwarded to Henry via the nursing home where she died rather than mailed to him direct. And it's in pencil. 'Pencil never counts,' insists a frantic daughter-in-law, mentally watching her husband's inheritance disappear. So does it even class as a letter? The Wilcoxes decide not: in the end, 'after due debate', they tear the note up and throw it on the dining-room fire. By the time Margaret hears about the bequest, on the last page of the novel, Henry has reduced it to the vague memory that his late wife had 'scribbled "Howards End" on a piece of paper when she wasn't herself'. The letter has, in effect, become 'unwritten'.

Yet the spirit of the note outlives the paper it was scribbled on and colours the rest of the novel. In a sort of cosmic justice, Howards End becomes Margaret's anyway, promised to her after Henry's death by a clause in his own will. And Margaret, realising that Mrs Wilcox had wanted her to have the house all along, responds to the silent 'rightness' of the outcome without bitterness at her husband's interference. The philosophical issue of whether or not the letter existed is no longer relevant: either way, Mrs Wilcox's wishes have been fulfilled.

Ignoring the second letter

JFK and Khrushchev during the Cuban Missile Crisis

President John F. Kennedy took a leaf out of the Wilcoxes' book when dealing with correspondence from Nikita Khrushchev during the Cuban Missile Crisis in 1962.

For 13 days in October that year, as Soviet missile launchpads multiplied on the island of Cuba, just 90 miles from the US, and Kennedy responded by surrounding it with a blockade of warships, the two superpowers seemed about to embark on a third world war. People who had lived through either of the first two knew this one would be apocalyptic (and my mother spent what must have been several months of her teacher's salary on a silver-grey sheepskin jacket that she'd been coveting in a shop window: if the world was going to end, she reckoned, there was no point worrying about making a hole in the housekeeping budget).

From Wednesday 24 October to Friday the 26th, Kennedy fended off his government and military advisers (most of whom wanted US forces to attack the Soviet bases) and just . . . did nothing, refusing to push Khrushchev into action and instead giving him enough time, he hoped, to make a conciliatory move. Desperate to avoid misunderstandings or mistakes, he held his nerve and waited. And at 7 p.m. on the 26th a long, rambling, emotional letter arrived by telegram from Moscow. The fourth volume of Robert Caro's biography of Lyndon Johnson, *The Passage of Power*, gives a gripping account of what happened next.

Although uncomfortably patronising in tone, the letter made it clear that Khrushchev was prepared to back down if he could do so without losing face. It was packed with conciliatory sentiments such as 'Let us not quarrel now; Let us show good sense; I consider these proposals reasonable', and it offered to dismantle the Soviet Union's Cuban installations in exchange for US assurances that it wouldn't invade Cuba. There were some irksome comments about Communists being the world's peacemakers, but the letter didn't ask much of the US in practical terms: just an undertaking not to invade Cuba or support anyone else's invasion. All JFK had to do was not let pride or ego (or his more hawkish advisers) deflect him from a path of calm pragmatism.

He hesitated too long, however, because the next day a second communication followed, this time a public letter, complete with the Embossed Seal of the USSR and copied to U Thant, Acting Secretary General of the UN. Barely half the length of the first, it was far more 'official' in tone and more alert, in its wording, to the public standing of the Soviet image. It made the Soviet pledges more binding, but at the same time made new, additional demands of the US. The no-invasion pledge asked for in the first letter was no longer enough: it now appeared that Russia's Cuban installations would only be dismantled if the US got rid of its own missile installations in Turkey as well. In fact, the US had been planning to remove these anyway (as the missiles were largely obsolete), but to do so in the wake of Khrushchev's public demand would look to the rest of the world like capitulation (and suggest an apparent willingness to sacrifice Turkey's security, too).

What now? Kennedy's solution was simply to act as though the second letter had never been received, and accept the terms of the first. His reply was handed in person to the Russian ambassador (along with a private offer to remove the Turkish missiles once the immediate crisis was resolved). On Sunday 28th, Khrushchev agreed the deal, and the threat of war rolled quietly away. The second letter – like Mrs Wilcox's bequest – was airbrushed out of the picture, as though it had never existed.

The unopened love letter

W. Somerset Maugham's *Mrs Craddock*

In Somerset Maugham's ruthless parable of class and sex, beautiful, headstrong Bertha Ley marries 'beneath her', and then becomes disillusioned with her husband when he metamorphoses from the unspoiled rustic she fell in love with into a stolid pillar of the establishment. The more successfully Edward Craddock wins over the doubters of her social circle, the less she likes him, until disappointment turns into loathing and she is tempted into an affair with a younger man – a distant cousin who is about to be sent to America as a punishment for 'philandering rather violently' with his mother's maid. Gerald is cheerfully, Byronically irresponsible, and Bertha can't resist his beauty and his passion, feeling herself too long deprived of both.

Gerald eventually leaves for America, pleading with her to let him stay longer – although not actually asking her to go with him (which is what she seems to want, in her distress on his last day). She soon starts to waver, however, between regret at not letting him stay and a conviction that he was worthless and that she's had a lucky escape: either way, it's probably enough passion and tumult to last her a lifetime.

After returning to her unsatisfactory husband, she receives a final letter from Gerald and tortures herself by imagining the contents before destroying it, still unread. Whether she had really loved him, or whether her attachment was just a craving for excitement, you can't help admiring that self-control, the refusal to give in to sentiment or curiosity, the way she resolutely shrinks it to the status of a non-letter.

> A feeling of anger seized her that the sight of a letter from Gerald should bring her such pain. She almost hated him now; and yet with all her heart she wished to kiss the paper and every word that was written upon it. But the violence of her emotion made her set her teeth, as it were, against giving way.
>
> 'I won't read it,' she said.
>
> She wanted to prove to herself that she had strength, and this temptation at least she was determined to resist. Bertha lit a candle and took the letter in her hand to burn it, but then put it down again. That would settle the matter too quickly, and she wanted rather to prolong the trial so as to receive full assurance of her fortitude. With a strange pleasure at the pain she was preparing for herself, Bertha placed the letter on the chimney-piece of her room, prominently, so that whenever she went in or out she could not fail to see it. Wishing to punish herself her desire was to make the temptation as distressing as possible.
>
> She watched the unopened envelope for a month, and sometimes the craving to open it was almost irresistible; sometimes she awoke in the middle of the night, thinking of Gerald, and told herself that she must know what he said. Ah, how well she could imagine it! He vowed he loved her, and he spoke of the kiss she had

given him on that last day, and he said it was dreadfully hard to be without her. Bertha looked at the letter, clenching her hands so as not to seize it and tear it open; she had to hold herself forcibly back from covering it with kisses. But at last she conquered all desire; she was able to look at the handwriting indifferently; she scrutinised her heart and found no trace of emotion. The trial was complete.

'Now it can go,' she said.

Again she lit a candle, and held the letter to the flame till it was all consumed; and she gathered up the ashes, putting them in her hand, and blew them out of the window. She felt that by that act she had finished with the whole thing, and that Gerald was definitely gone out of her life.

‘You can’t send that!’

William Boyd’s *The Dreams of Bethany Mellmoth*

Novelists have their own escape routes for uncomfortable thoughts: they can make their characters mouthpieces for feelings they want to vent. But that doesn’t make them any less prone to resentments of their own. William Boyd, interviewed for the *Sunday Times* in October 2017, admitted that he gets things out of his system by writing letters that his wife then prevents him from sending. ‘When I’m fed up I usually write letters of death to whoever’s wounded me, but then I show them to Susan who says, “You can’t send that!”’ Generally, he points out, your best weapon against those who have riled you is ‘utter indifference’. (For more letters written as Therapy, or not sent because Thought Better Of, see chapters III and IV.)

Boyd worked his own habit into the character of failed writer Yves Hill, who first appeared in a 2004 short story called ‘The View from Yves Hill’ and re-surfaces via several linked plotlines in the 2017 collection *The Dreams of Bethany Mellmoth*. In the story ‘Humiliation’, Yves is suddenly confronted, on a motoring tour of France (because he’s been reduced to writing badly paid travel features), with one of the critics who has savaged his latest novel, *Oblong*. At first, he tries to practise Boyd’s policy of ‘utter indifference’, but he finds he can’t stay indifferent, and his trip is now infused with thoughts of revenge. Before he hits on the idea of shellfish poisoning (revenge being, in this case, best served dubiously warm), and realising that the critic is holidaying with a mistress, he mentally pens a 'short deadly letter' to the man's wife: 'Dear Mrs Maltravers, Last week, your husband was in Sainte-Radegonde, Dordogne, accompanied by a woman. Sincerely, a Friend.' The letter remains unwritten as, happy in the knowledge that he has the power to ruin Maltravers's life, he can afford to let him enjoy his mistress for a few days more.

But in the subsequent story, actually titled 'Unsent Letters', Yves is writing – and not sending – letters for a different reason. He's by this time become a film-maker, and the plot of *Oblong* is now a doomed film project called *Oblong or Triangle*. No longer attempting to feign indifference, he drafts letter after letter to producers, actors and agents in the movie business – as well as to the bank manager he sees as frustrating his efforts. All broken off mid-sentence – either in despair at their futility or because Yves has thought of a better argument, a more useful recipient – they become increasingly, furiously frantic, the ramblings of a fantasist.

We don't know whether they were early versions of letters actually sent, or therapeutic rants being composed in his head and never put down on paper, or whether he eventually made his approach to the various addressees by phone or email instead. But the irony is that he frequently stresses the significance of an 'old-fashioned letter rather than an email', a chance to 'set things down in black and white'. (Whereas of course the truth is that if it had been an email he probably *would* have sent it, would have pressed the button in rage or drunkenness or incompetence.)

1 March

Dear Meryl,

We haven't met but, as you can see from my letterhead, I am a film director and producer (Flaming Terrapin Productions Ltd). I thought I would write an old-fashioned letter rather than an email, if only to show ~~how much an admirer I am of you~~ how much importance I attach to this communication. In fact, we have a mutual friend in the shape of Tarquin Wolde, my co-producer – whom I believe you worked with, or were about to work with, on *Jezebel* – before the whole thing collapsed. What a business!

Anyhoo, I wanted to send you the script of my latest film, *Oblong or Triangle*, in the genuine hope that you'd consider playing the co-lead role of 'Ernestine' – above the title, of course. If you were interested, at all, I'd be prepared to travel the world to meet you (I'll be in New York next month, as it happens). Nothing would give me greater pleasure than –

2 March

My darling Jadranka,

How I miss you, my sweet girl. I miss you so much I thought I'd write to you, rather than call. Set things down in black and white, not rely on those transient, shifting things that are words, spoken. How are matters

> in sunny Pietermaritzburg? I hope that bastard Tim Whatsisname is treating you well. He's a lecherous swine, so be careful – and don't make him force you to do night-shoots. He deliberately tries to exhaust his actors, so I've been told, to make them more vulnerable to his advances. And don't be alone with him. ~~He flashed his cock at Paula Vanni in a script meeting.~~ Just keep your distance – and keep mentioning my name – he absolutely knows who I am. Call me your 'fiancé' (well, I am, sort of!). Darling, I wanted to write because it looks very much as if the shoot of *Oblong or Triangle* isn't going to happen in June, after all. The usual boring financial issues. We will definitely be going in the Fall so I want you to keep yourself available – if anyone can pull this off, I can, don't worry. I have hopes that Meryl (!) might play 'Ernestine' – negotiations are underway. What do you think about a week in Capri when your shoot ends? Let me know and I'll book a suite in –

And by September, he's given up the movie business and has accepted a position as Professor of Film and Media Studies at the University of Shoreditch ('~~Quite a good salary, long holidays, moderate teaching load~~', he explains in another unsent letter to Jadranka).

'You are an old goose'

The virtual world of *The Complete Letter Writer for Ladies & Gentlemen*

From an age when life was conducted through written correspondence, here are letters that will never now be sent, and perhaps never were (and many others that really, honestly shouldn't be). Routledge's *Complete Letter Writer for Ladies & Gentlemen* was 1939's answer to a self-help manual. Entire lives – complete with names, addresses and personal details – are plotted through templates covering every potential circumstance: money to be lent, invitations accepted and declined, church bazaars manned and wills witnessed.

Herbert F. Lemon of Putney complains to his neighbour, Horace M. Crispin, about a barking dog, a daughter's early-morning piano practice and Mr and Mrs Crispin's habit of holding noisy conversations in their garden. Muriel Butler-Conroy of London writes to Mrs Barton in Dorset to introduce friends who are moving near her: a splendid-sounding all-round athlete and Cricket Blue who is also an authority on Swine Fever, and a wife who used to play the violin 'when she was younger and had time to practise'. People congratulate each other on their sons' (never daughters') exam results and headmasters give parents advice concerning their children's careers (for one boy who is 'agreeable' but not particularly clever, a lawyer's office is recommended).

Most poignant of all are the letter templates for young men and women in love – and the recommended responses, both favourable and not. These include:

> LETTER OF PROPOSAL FROM A GENTLEMAN TO A YOUNG LADY HE HAS MET ONLY ON A FEW OCCASIONS. (Favourable reply: 'Dear Albert, I already feel as if I had known you for years.' Angry reply: 'Sir, You have greatly misjudged me if you consider I will tolerate such liberties.')

and

> LETTER FROM A GIRL TO HER FATHER ANNOUNCING HER ENGAGEMENT. (Favourable reply: 'My dear Edith, I have always liked Jack. I consider him an upright and manly fellow, and a very capable man of business.' Unfavourable reply: 'My dear Edith, I cannot help saying that your news has given me great uneasiness. I am bound to admit that I do not like Jack Fisher.')

The book's hypothetical situations – and its resulting letters – become increasingly specific and bizarre. Picture the characters involved in the following exchange (and the future prognosis for their relationship):

LETTER FROM A GENTLEMAN COMPLAINING OF THE CONDUCT OF HIS FIANCEE

19 Rose Hill,
Sydenham, SW,

Dear Julia,

As you know I am not at all a jealous person, and I am not one of the people who think that an engaged girl should talk to no other man but her fiancé, but I must say I am quite at a loss to know how to take your recent conduct. Last night you scarcely took any notice of me whatsoever, but reserved it all for young Higgens, who, as you must be perfectly aware, is a notorious flirt and altogether worthless. I could not help overhearing several people remarking on it. You can imagine what I felt like! Dear Julia, if you are repenting of our engagement you had much better tell me; on the other hand, if it is merely thoughtlessness on your part, I must tell you that you are trying me very much. I hope you will forgive my saying all this.

Ever your affectionate,

Alfred.

CONCILIATORY REPLY

2 Hallow Avenue,
Sydenham, SW,

My dearest Alf,

You are an old goose. Your letter has made me laugh and cry by turns. Surely you must know that you are the only person I care for. If you don't like Bill Higgens, I certainly won't take any more notice of him. He certainly struck me as rather amusing, but that was all. I had no idea that I had been cold to you last night. You struck me as silent, so I thought it best not to bother you. Come round here tonight.

Always your,

Julia.

UNCONCILIATORY REPLY

2 Hallow Avenue,
Sydenham, SW,

Dear Alf,

Your letter seems to me very unnecessary. You say that you are not jealous, and then proceed to give a remarkable example of jealousy on your part. Really, if you are going to write me letters like this it would be perhaps as well if we did reconsider our engagement. I spoke to Mr Higgens, because he was amusing and witty. I avoided you because you were sulky. It is very absurd of you to suppose that I am going to follow you like a tame cat. Like everybody else, I like to get some enjoyment and freedom.

Julia.

And, from the *Complete Letter Writer*'s list of ten golden rules, two to take particular note of:

1) Think before you write. A letter, once posted, is the property of the Postmaster-General, till it is delivered to the addressee. You cannot overtake it; therefore, do not let regret overtake you.

And

2) Many letters answer themselves. An angry letter is seldom worth its postage.

'An Unposted Letter'

Iris Barry

Iris Barry (1895-1969) was a British-born film critic, novelist and poet. Her circle of friends in 1920s literary London included Ezra Pound, Wyndham Lewis (with whom she had two children) and the American poet Alan Porter, whom she married. She co-founded the London Film Society, created the Film Library at the Museum of Modern Art in New York and served on the jury of the first Cannes Film Festival in 1946.

How bitter must the smile
Of the wise Future be
Behind her veil!
O letter of last year,
Can my hopes and aims,
  Like moons,
Have changed so?
Those dead desires,
Like shrivelled fruits,
Hang, shamed,
On the bough of time.